CHOCOLATE

CHOCOLATE

Mariarosa Schiaffino

With illustrations by Franco Testa

MICHAEL JOSEPH

First published in Great Britain in 1989 by
Webb & Bower (Publishers) Limited,
9 Colleton Crescent, Exeter, Devon EX2 4BY,
in association with Michael Joseph Limited,
27 Wright's Lane, London W8 5TZ

Penguin Books Ltd, Registered Offices: Harmondsworth,
Middlesex, England
Penguin Books Australia Ltd, Ringwood, Victoria, Australia
Penguin Books Canada Ltd, 2801 John Street, Markham, Ontario,
Canada L3R 1D4
Penguin Books (NZ) Ltd, 182–190 Wairau Road, Auckland 10, New Zealand

Designed by Carlotta Maderna / Vic Giolitto
Series Editor Mariarosa Schiaffino
With illustrations by Franco Testa

Translated from the Italian by Kerry Milis
Copyright © 1985 Idealibri SpA, Milan
Copyright © 1989 Idealibri SpA, Milan, for English translation

British Library Cataloguing in Publication Data

Schiaffino, Mariarosa
Chocolate.
1. Chocolate
I. Title II. series III. Cioccolao &
Cioccolatini. *English*
641.3'374
ISBN 0–86350–293–8

Typeset in Great Britain by Scribes, Exeter, Devon

Printed and bound in Italy by Grafiche Editoriali Ambrosiane di Milano

CONTENTS

INTRODUCTION
THE STUFF OF DREAMS

'A DREAM is a wish your heart makes', goes Cinderella's song. Dreams are the stuff of childhood games. We turn to them when we are told to sit quietly, not to move and to keep our voices down, and we turn to them when we cannot fall asleep at night.

I used to play such games, to dream such daydreams. I remember one in particular. You had to think of something beautiful, really beautiful, something that did not exist, that each of us, sisters and friends, would like to receive as a present. And you had to describe it down to the last detail, in the most tantalizing and convincing terms so we would all want it.

For my sister, it was always an incredibly beautiful dress, like her Cinderella gown in every shade of blue with a skirt made of fluffy clouds. For me it was fantasies of confectionery, the most delicious sweets, a bed of spun sugar, and – even now I can still see it – the Chocolate Schoolbag.

It had numerous compartments and an enormous handle, just like the one I used to take to school, but was made of dark chocolate. I would open it and instead of books, notebooks and pencil cases, out would tumble a cascade of shiny, wrapped chocolates and all kinds of bars in different flavours. It was the schoolbag of my dreams, the symbol of my single-minded and all-consuming passion for chocolate. That's the way it was then and that's the way it still is, in spite of the guilty feelings that still plague me when I wantonly abandon myself to the call of this irresistible food with only one drawback: that it is too delicious.

My innocent childish dream of a solid chocolate schoolbag came to mind with great clarity when I recently visited a chocolate factory and saw, with astonishment, how the exquisite substance, when it hardens, can take on any shape. It only needs a mould for this dark, perfumed splendour to become the magic evidence of hyperbole, a dramatic surrealist truth.

Today, I could have my Chocolate Schoolbag . . .

CHAPTER I

In the Heart, on the Tongue

Viva chocolate and whoever invented it!

Carlo Goldoni (1707–1793), from La conversazione

CHOCOLATE has claimed the attention of gourmets and gourmands for centuries, but recently psychologists have begun to consider it too. It is a substance that seems to have been made purposely for subtle and alluring interpretations. Are you hopelessly in love with chocolate? A psychologist might say that you are rewarding the childish part of your self, that is to say, the eternal child voluptuously going back to the maternal breast each time you reach into a box of chocolates or sink your teeth into the sweetness of a dark perfumed bar. Not to mention emotional compensation – chocolate as substitute for the affection denied us in childhood or perhaps lost (in which case the theory is that devouring chocolate is part of the 'mourning process'). Chocolate, then, is a replacement for, or at least about surviving in the hopes of, love.

So far so good, but in that case I cannot help feeling sorry for the Swiss, or for the thousands of Swedes driven to the arms of this dark consolation. The statistics are clear. The English are heavy consumers of chocolate, 16½lb/7.5kg per person per year, while Americans consume 11¼lb/5kg. But look at the poor Swiss who consume 21¾lb/9.9kg per year and the Swedish with 19¾lb/9kg. Belgians, too, have their problems, weighing in at 16¾lb/7.7kg, while the Germans average 15½lb/7kg and the French 11lb/5kg. The Italians only manage 2¾lb/1.3kg a year. For most Europeans and Americans, then, chocolate is a food of the people, consumed by the masses, and not Theobroma, 'the food of the gods', as Linnaeus baptized the cacao tree.

Quite apart from my feelings of compassion for the millions of people with so many complexes and so little love, I must point out another less spiritual and more mundane side to all this. Although things have changed in the last decade, in the Scandinavian countries chocolate, like sweets in general, has tended to be an integral part of a normal diet, very rich in the fats and sugars that used to be considered helpful protection against the cold winters of the north. It is not only reserved for special occasions and parties, to be offered as a show of hospitality, it is not necessarily treated as a special gift or prize, nor does it bestow any special privilege or sign of affection on the receiver.

For Germans, Norwegians, Belgians, or the English, eating chocolate is a perfectly normal thing to do. For Mediterraneans, on the other hand, who have a different diet, it is looked upon as a sign of indulgence, a gesture of pleasure, to such an extent that people are often a bit ashamed to be seen eating it in public, as if it were a sign of weakness or ostentation – or even worse, a lack of virility, albeit a childish one . . .

Fortunately, though, there are many happy to declare loudly their love for the exquisite Theobroma and who try to convert others. Ruggero De Daninos, an Italian actor and poet, writes about chocolate. Not only is he truly in love with the stuff, he has taken to the radio waves to proclaim his hopeless rapture when confronted with the 'famous silver paper', the seductive lamé wrappings of that gorgeous perfumed object. He says, 'Once the resplendent wrapping has been removed, the smooth, creamy brown skin is revealed, inviting caresses. Finally, there is its sweet body, pliable, warm, soft, flexible, docile . . . faced with which all thoughts of chastity are lost . . .'

Presented with such ardour, a psychologist would comment: 'Here we have a person who is not afraid to show their childish side, a person who has the courage to spoil themself and admit it publicly.' Furthermore, the psychologist would say, 'this cherished object, as alluring as Eros, is in reality the image of the mother figure, an hypnotic suggestion to mind and senses taking us back to the maternal breast'.

So, are we talking about nothing more profound than overgrown children with sweet tooths? Maybe. Nevertheless, there are certain extremists among them who are perpetually in love and like anyone in love, willing to go any distance for the beloved Theobroma.

This group of lovers, in fact, constitutes a new category among chocolate lovers in general, the chocolate addict. They are especially prevalent – it seems – in certain Anglo-Saxon countries to the north.

Like a Drug

Torment and ecstasy, sin and temptation, intoxication and perdition: not excessive words for a substance like chocolate.

History is constantly confirming this. In all periods of history and in every culture, people have felt a visceral and inescapable love for chocolate: Goethe, Napoleon, Hitler, all bear witness to this, but it is not hard to find victims, even chocolate addicts in everyday life as well. However, they are clever, often hiding their insane passion, jealously cultivating it in private. They only feel they have been unmasked when someone by chance catches them sticking their fingers into a delicious chocolate cream pie or sitting in front of a small mountain of candy wrappers, the irrefutable evidence of a frenetic and delicious ritual. Indeed, chocolate addicts are coming to be considered in the same class as drug addicts.

For chocolate addicts, an unquenchable desire can suddenly manifest itself in a tormenting fashion: they 'need' a chocolate bar or a box of chocolates and they need it now; if they are forced to go without the supreme food, then at a pinch, a cake will do. They may even (how low they sometimes stoop!) be reduced to scouting the neighbourhood for the nearest newstand, underground station vending machine, local café or pub. The quality is not always so good in these impulse buys (whose consumption nevertheless is undergoing an incredible increase), but in those desperate moments, they will do. Those subject to frequent withdrawal symptoms keep provisions in their homes for any emergency and they keep them carefully hidden. When the moment arrives when they feel their wild and crazy desire, there is fast relief at hand.

The owner of a fine California restaurant confesses that occasionally when all the customers have gone home and he is at last alone, he receives enormous pleasure from going into the deserted kitchen, cutting a chunk of chocolate from the giant blocks he buys for use in one of the restaurant's favourite desserts, and eating the whole thing all by himself: 'Chocolate has such an intense, powerful taste that it gives me great joy. It is not unusual for me to celebrate to the limits and open a bottle of champagne. There is no better marriage.'

Chocolate on the Tongue

Everything about chocolate is pleasurable. Even its name has a certain fascination. We might not know what it smells like or what its indescribable flavour is, but just the musical pronunciation of the word with its energetic

'ch' at the beginning, sweet and drawling at the end, can be enough to light the flames of fantasy and build up our hopes.

The name comes from the Aztec word '*xocolatl*' and according to the English missionary Thomas Gage, who referred to it around 1648, this is an onomatopoeic word. Its ending '*atle*' or '*atte*' means 'water' in the ancient Mexican language, and according to his understanding the Aztecs added '*choc*' or '*xoc*' because it is like the sound that the drink produces when it is beaten 'until it forms bubbles and foam' or when it is stirred.

Our word 'chocolate' comes from '*xocolatl*' through the Spanish word '*chocolate*' and in fact the word is very similar in almost all the almost three hundred or so languages of the world. The same is true of the word 'cocoa'.

Research carried out by the Dutch scholar Italiaander, the author of two rigorous volumes on this delicious subject, gives us this interesting panorama of Europe:

English	cocoa	chocolate
Spanish	cacao	chocolate
Portuguese	cacau	chocolate
Italian	cacao	cioccolato
French	cacao	chocolat
Dutch	cacao	chocolat
Belgian	cacao	chocolade
German	cacao	Schokolade
Danish	kakao	Chocolade
Norwegian	kakao	sjokolade (old form, '*chocolade*')
Swedish	kakao	choklad
Polish	kakao	zsekolada
Rumanian	cacao	ciocolata
Czech	kakao	cokolade
Hungarian	kakao	csokolade
Estonian	kakao	shokolade
Lithuanian	kakao	sokolade
Finnish	kaakao	suklaa

Juan Corominas, a Spanish linguist and the author of the *Etymological Dictionary of the Castilian Language*, attributes the origin of the word to the Aztecs and he makes the following hypothesis: since the oldest records on the preparation of this concoction say that the ancient Mexicans made it with the seed of the silk-cotton tree (*pochotl*) and the cocoa tree (*cacauatl*) perhaps the word 'chocolate' comes from '*pocho-cacaua-atl*', drink from cocoa and silk-cotton, shortened by the Spanish to '*chocauatl*'. In its present form the word may also have had a phonetic influence on other Mexican drinks like '*pocolatl*', a drink made from cooked maize, '*pinolatl*', a drink from pinenuts, and '*chilatl*', a Chilean drink.

CHAPTER II
DRINK OF THE GODS

The gods drink ambrosia, people drink chocolate.

G B Anfossi, from The Use and Abuse of Chocolate, *1779*

THERE was a period in European history when the Old World seemed to be dominated by a thirst never before felt, a thirst for new sensations, for unknown flavours and smells, for exotic drinks. This was the period between the sixteenth and seventeenth centuries. From steaming pots, potions were poured into cups at all hours of the day and these were drunk to restore the spirit and awaken the palate. People believed these potions exuded beneficial and stimulating vapours, helping them to think clearly, improving conversation, elevating the spirit, and giving new meaning to the art of gallantry.

Coffee, tea and chocolate all came to Europe from different distant countries during an era of great explorations and the adventurous conquests of far-off lands. The first came from the Arab countries, the second from China and the third from the Americas. Three drinks that were considered 'for company' and which contributed decisively to the formation in distinguished society of a new way of drinking, of convivially passing the time, of exchanging ideas and discussing politics.

Tea was a subtle, contemplative, metaphysical drink; coffee was animating, stimulating, invigorating; chocolate was the voluptuous drink, energizing but sensual. Women were the first to fall in love with it. When Anne of Austria, a Spanish princess, married Louis XIII of France in 1615, she was still a girl, but even then she had clearly defined tastes and she refused to give up the chocolate she had brought with her from her native country. Once launched in the French court, the fashion for chocolate spread to the rest of Europe.

The path chocolate took in Europe had begun in Spain where it had arrived from the New World on Hernan Cortes's ships. But its history goes back even further.

Columbus discovers Chocolate

The first Europeans to discover the cacao tree and its fruit seem to have been Columbus's men on his fourth voyage of exploration, between 1502 and 1504. Reaching the island of Guanaja off the Honduras coast, the Spanish ships saw coming towards them a canoe propelled by twenty-four oarsmen. The oarsmen were carrying merchandise, weapons, cloth and pottery, and they had also brought some small beans that they used as currency – even today they are used as such in remote villages. These beans were from the cacao tree, but of course the Spanish sailors did not know this nor could they have imagined the treasure these beans hid. Perhaps they did wonder why they were considered so valuable, but the matter went no further at that stage.

Quetzalcoatl's Gift

According to botanists, the cacao tree was already growing freely four thousand years before Christ in the Orinoco and Amazon river basins.

Through tribal migrations, it was introduced into the Yucatan peninsula in Mexico long before the modern era. When the Mayas went south, they took it with them into the lands that were later occupied by the Toltecs, the people who came before the Aztecs in Central American history.

The eventual Aztec domination of the area led to an enormous empire of worshippers of the Sun, and of the Plumed Serpent – the god 'Quetzalcoatl', founder of the race. The Aztecs believed that it was Quetzalcoatl who had created cacao as a divine gift to relieve fatigue and provide a pleasurable rest. The fruit of the tree was so valuable that conquered tribes were forced to pay tribute in beans to the representatives of the imperial powers, while for ten beans the rich could buy a rabbit and for twelve, a courtesan.

Like all plants with a social and symbolic importance (for instance, tea, which Buddhists believe came from the eyelids of the Bodidharma), cacao was believed to be of divine origin.

An Aztec legend tells of a princess who was left to watch over a great treasure belonging to her husband who had gone off to defend the borders of the empire. While he was away, she was attacked by his enemies who tried in vain to make her reveal the place where the treasure was hidden. As revenge for her silence, they killed her and from her blood sprouted the cacao plant whose fruit hid a great treasure in its seeds, which were as bitter as the sufferings of love, as strong as virtue and as red as blood. Cacao was Quetzalcoatl's gift for the woman's faithfulness to her husband even unto death, the same faithfulness that the subjects of the enormous Aztec empire professed to their emperor.

Apart from the legend, clearly cocoa played an essential role in religious rites. The Mayas believed that the beverage they made by toasting and grinding the seeds would nourish them after death. The Aztecs believed that a cup of *xocolatl* banished fatigue and stimulated their psychic and mental abilities.

The Return of the Plumed Serpent

The great god Quetzalcoatl was an absent god. He had abandoned his people millions of years earlier after another false and evil king had defeated him. But he had sworn that some day he would return to seek revenge and he would again rule the Aztecs with all the splendour of the past. Quetzalcoatl, the white god of a dark race, had promised that he would return by sea. In 1519 when Cortes's ships reached Mexico and bearded white men disembarked, the Aztecs were convinced that Quetzalcoatl had returned. The white god had finally arrived from the sea! Montezuma, the emperor and high priest, personally received Cortes's soldiers and he rendered homage to their captain, offering him, among other gifts, the dark spicy drink called *xocolatl*. Cortes wrote:

Montezuma was the king of a rich and powerful country. The Spanish could not help but admire the abundance and luxury in which he lived: . . . beautifully worked exquisite dishes; . . . fifty pots of foamy cocoa which were brought for him to taste and which would be drunk afterwards . . .

Under Spanish domination the peasants continued to eat corn and drink *xocolatl*. It allowed them to march for hours along the tortuous mountain roads and bear up under the hard work of the harvest without feeling so deeply their fatigue. The Spanish began to realize why this plant and its drink was considered so valuable and from that moment on, chocolate and the cocoa bean became a part of their own diet.

The Cacaute

Cortes returned to Spain in 1528 bringing with him fruit from the cacao tree. It immediately provoked great interest among botanists. It inspired Girolamo Benzoni for one to travel to America in 1541 and 1555 and to write *Historia del Mondo Nuovo*, published in Venice in 1565. At first the Spanish considered *cacaute* 'food for pigs rather than for men', Benzoni relates, '. . . wishing on certain occasions to give me something to drink and I, not wishing to accept it, the natives, very astonished, went away laughing'. But later, he says, 'lacking wine, having always to drink water, I did as the others. Its flavour is somewhat bitter, it quenches thirst and refreshes the body, but it does not produce drunkenness . . . A gourd filled with this piquant liquid sustains and comforts . . .'

Bitter, yes, but as with most things there was a solution. The Spanish had introduced the cultivation of sugar cane over large areas, from the Canary Islands to Santo Domingo and Mexico. Someone had the marvellous idea of adding sugar to the drink, another of adding aniseed, cinnamon and vanilla, and voila! *cacaute* was transformed into a delicious drink, a true gift of the gods.

The first chocolate shops were opened in Mexico, even before Spain, and they were heavily patronized by the Spanish who sipped the refreshing velvety drink while they listened to music and dreamed of their far-off mother land. The use of sweetened chocolate soon spread to Venezuela and the other conquered territories and from there reached Europe and Spain.

Just as with the ancient Aztecs, chocolate quickly became a food for kings, reserved for the court and considered of great value. Famous monasteries chosen for their pharmaceutical abilities were selected to prepare it. Then, there was another discovery: chocolate was even better served hot.

Hot, fragrant, sweet: there was hardly anything left to connect it with the 'savage' beverage which was drunk cold, thick, foamy and unsweetened and flavoured with herbs, vanilla, pepper and other spices. Throughout the sixteenth century the dark ambrosia won new followers. It might almost be said that when the Spanish introduced it into Flanders, their conquest of Europe had begun.

The First Successes

Meanwhile, others were working to break Spain's monopoly. The first to succeed was a Florentine, Fran-

Colonists, priests and Indians from a book written by Thomas Gage in the first half of the seventeenth century

cesco Carletti, an observant traveller and scrupulous narrator. Carletti visited the plantations and afterwards described how the Indians prepared the cocoa beans and how they made the drink – by crushing the beans with water and – by then – sugar. It was then served in a cup, 'stirred mainly with a small stick, that was rotated with the palms of their hands, to produce a red foam'. Carletti added that the cocoa when it solidified in blocks was taken on voyages as a food and when necessary it was dissolved in water and afterwards, 'drunk in one gulp'. Carletti seems to have been one of the first to import some of the fruit of these plants for commercial use. This was the beginning of chocolate's modern history, when it began to be consumed in Europe as a drink or in solid form as confectionery.

Enthusiasms and Doubts

By 1606 chocolate was being made in Italy. Chocolate makers were very skilful and were highly esteemed in Florence and Venice and after that in other countries, where many went to seek their fortunes.

France was the first to adopt the exotic beverage with zeal. Cardinal Richelieu's brother and Queen Maria Theresa, wife of Louis XIV after 1659, were both great chocolate lovers. But as Braudel tells it, chocolate at that time was considered a medicine as well as a food and it had not yet taken its place as a drink of pleasure and hospitality.

In the seventeenth century, the Dutch, who were great navigators, took over Spain's cocoa monopoly and gained control of the world market. They brought the precious beans from America, stopping along the way in the Spanish ports and continuing on to their own country where cocoa was eagerly awaited by chocolate lovers and recommended by famous doctors as a cure for almost every ailment.

Chocolate reached Germany probably in 1646 thanks to a student from Nuremberg, Johann Georg Volkammer, who had developed a taste for it in Naples. However, it was heavily taxed by the government, so that only a few were able to enjoy it.

A few years later, in 1657, the English discovered

chocolate. Initially considered an extravagance and thus limited to the privileged few, it came to be enjoyed more widely when shops for its consumption were opened. In 1647, for example, a famous London café, At the Coffee Mill and Tobacco Roll, offered its clients a chocolate drink and also sold it in solid form, 'Spanish-style'.

Finally it was the turn of the Zurich burgomaster Henry Hescher to discover chocolate during a visit to Brussels. When he returned home he served it to his friends who in turn served it to their friends. This is the way things often spread, but no one could have imagined what a brilliant future awaited chocolate in that small country.

Meanwhile in Paris, in the court of Philip of Orleans, 'to go for chocolate', to be present at the prince's break-fast, became a synonym for being in favour with him, and the court developed a true passion for the aromatic drink.

However, in the background, there were voices of alarm. Madame de Sevigny commented on the latest craze in her correspondence with her daughter. At first, she was in its favour, but then, after two months, she confessed, 'Fashion has swept me away as usual. Now everyone speaks badly of it because it is like a constant fever in the body . . .' In October 1671, the famous lady advised her daughter not to be too indulgent with the drink: 'The Marquise of Coetlogon drank so much chocolate during her pregnancy that her baby was born as black as the devil and soon died . . .'

Black as the Devil

The colour of chocolate held a dangerous attraction: it was that of the devil. While it may also have been the colour of monks' habits, it was also the colour of the pagan Indians' skin and in its darkest form that of the devil himself. Perhaps this was why the drink seemed to carry with it undertones of vice and sin, 'almost a form of hidden drunkenness, a tenacious habit', wrote Alberto Capatti. As Carletti had already noted, it was one which pardoned no one, 'among the religious and among important people'. In fact, chocolate was highly regarded in ecclesiastic circles. It became so important that a

dispute broke out among the clergy which risked destroying the unity of the Church.

With the Blessings of the Cardinal

Can chocolate be drunk on days of abstinence? Does it or does it not break the fast? Such subtle questions caused great controversy in their day.

An ordinance from Pope Pius V in 1569 established that *'liquida non frangunt jejunum'* ('liquids do not break the fast'), but could the dense velvety chocolate be defined as a liquid with a clear conscience? Spanish women had taken up the habit of drinking chocolate immediately after mass. Originally Aztec servants had carried the steaming pots to the temples for the pleasure

Cardinal Lorenzo Brancaccio who 'absolved' chocolate and its followers

of pious women; in Spain, priests were substituted for the servants and the morning ritual became a moment of distraction for the ladies and their spiritual fathers. The Church leaders tried to prohibit this practice but the clergy rebelled, and intellectuals and theologians suddenly were found debating the nature of the aromatic beverage.

Finally someone came up with a solution to the controversy that satisfied everyone: he was Cardinal Brancaccio whose logic was as subtle as his morals were light. Going back to an Aristotelian definition, in 1662 he qualified chocolate as a drink '*per accidens*' but it was still a drink and as such had to be considered like water and wine and admitted into the sacristy. As it happened, the high prelate also had a personal interest in the problem: a great devotee of chocolate, he had dedicated a long ode to it, which while perhaps not very beautiful, was inspired and sincere.

Another Jesuit, the Neopolitan Tommaso Strozzi, composed a poem on chocolate in 1786 that testified to his enthusiasm in each of its more than three hundred verses in Latin:

> My lips eagerly approach
> The foaming cup
> They skim over the divine liquid
> And sip it.
> what flavour it has!
> What a dewy new morning!
> Does such ambrosia exist?
> That delights the palate more?

While the gluttonous ministers of God glorified the dark elixir, in the cold Northern regions Swedes were looking at the cocoa bean with scientific eyes. Linnaeus gave the name of 'Theobroma' to the substance, a name suggestive of its origins as the favourite food of the gods.

CHAPTER III

ARISTOCRATIC REFRESHMENT, BOURGEOIS SNACK

> 'What do you do for mortification during Lent?' asked the confessor.
> 'Instead of coffee with milk, I have chocolate, which I prefer,' replied the penitent.
>
> *Giulio Piccini, in the* Almanacco Gastronomico

'SHH-H-H! Don't make any noise. I know it's almost eleven, but Madame has still not got up.'
Finally a ray of light makes its way through the top of the shutters and the whine of a puppy in the alcove pulls Madame from her dreams and returns her to the bustle of mundane appointments that make up her day.

In the semi-darkness of the room, full of the drowsiness of the night, she opens the curtains, sticks out her head, still wearing her nightcap, and rings the bell. A young maid comes in carrying a tray with the first cup of chocolate of the day, her wake-up cup.

The lady puts her lips to the fragrant nectar. In the other room, in the boudoir, hairdressers, tailors, dancing instructors and lovers are waiting.

This scene written in the nineteenth century by the Goncourt brothers, who were fascinated by the spirit and customs of the eighteenth century, the Age of Enlightenment, of reason and gallantry, reflects the beginning of a typical day in the life of a lady of leisure. It also depicts the period when the enjoyment of hot chocolate was at its peak. A substantial drink that did not sit heavily on the stomach, it was sipped in cafés and salons, in courts and in private clubs. Shaped and mixed with orange peel and dried fruits, chocolate was included in the precious box of sweets that was an indispensable part of elegant life. It was eaten with pleasure and passed around while playing cards or chatting, savoured while out for a drive in the carriage, sucked on during an evening's entertainment.

Not even a discreet midnight supper, the latest fad of

Chocolate for breakfast in an eighteenth-century French engraving

the fashionable for amorous meetings, could take place without chocolate. In contrast to tea and even more so to coffee, it went perfectly with the headiness of sparkling wine that seemed so appropriate for love. In fact it was usually a fundamental part of the ritual because women adored it. An italian book on etiquette for noble youths published in 1751 recommended that a gentlemen should always carry two white handkerchiefs with him, 'one for peeling fruit, the other for serving a woman when she has a sorbet, coffee or chocolate . . .' Clearly, life was sweet for those who had time and money to enjoy it.

The First Commercial Chocolate Makers

During the eighteenth century while cocoa plantations were spreading over Brazil, Martinique and the Philippines, chocolate making was developing in various European cities.

A valuable document that records an important moment in the history of chocolate has been preserved in the archives in Turin. It is dated 1678 and it concerns the concession that 'Madama Reale' gave to one G Antonio Ari who had made a petition to 'sell in public chocolate as a drink for the next six years from the date of the present document'.

'We have agreed with pleasure,' says the document, 'to your petition to be the first provider.' So it was that Mr Ari was allowed to be the first to introduce the drink of cocoa in Turin and there were soon famous chocolate makers who followed him in the Via Doragrossa, on the Contrada Accademia, on the Contrada Nuova.

By the end of the seventeenth century, Turin was one of the European capitals of chocolate. It made 750 pounds/340 kilos of chocolate a day and exported it to Austria, Switzerland, Germany and France. Cocoa was brought by Manuel Filibert of Savoy, general of the Spanish armies. Although he was not very well loved by history, he should receive everlasting recognition from all chocolate lovers.

Even today, Turin and the Piedmont region still carry on the art of chocolate making with great passion and drinking hot chocolate continues to be a popular pastime.

The End of the Artisan Era

At the beginning of the eighteenth century, the most famous chocolate makers in Paris were David Chaillou in rue L'Arbre Sec, 'Sieur' Rere in the Place Dauphine and another manufacturer, 'Sieur' Renaud, who composed a little song as an advertisement:

> *Pour l'avoir agréable*
> *allez chez Renaud l'acheter.*
> *On l'y trouve admirable.*

Chocolate triumphed throughout the whole century. Marie Antoinette, famous for loving cake, but who at heart preferred simplicity, liked chocolate with sugar and vanilla with none of the other flavourings that often adorned it. Her personal chocolate maker prepared what she called 'health chocolate' which was not very different from the kind we like today.

Everything, from the harvesting of the cacao beans to the finished product, was still done by hand. However, efforts were beginning to be made to facilitate and mechanize at least some aspects of the different phases of preparation: a certain Dubuisson for example, substituted the board shown in the drawing, on which the worker knelt to grind the beans, for a heated horizontal plank at which someone could work standing up much

Chocolate making in a small shop in the eighteenth century: an employee is crushing the beans on a tilted board

more comfortably. In 1778 a hydraulic machine was set up in Paris to crush the beans; but it was in Barcelona in 1777 where a Señor Fernandez was given the title of 'Manufacturer of Chocolate for Madame the Delphin and their Highnesses the Princes of the Courts' for producing chocolate mechanically for the first time.

After this the period of completely handmade chocolate, almost two glorious centuries of chocolate making, was over forever. The French Revolution and the political unrest at the end of the eighteenth century slowed industrial progress, but at the beginning of the nineteenth century, as the cocoa plantations developed around the world, the chocolate industry grew more organized and improvements were carried out in various countries. Let's look at the most important developments.

One of the first allowed chocolate to solidify so it could be shaped into a block. The Turin chocolate makers vied for supremacy in this process, using an invention by a certain Bozelli, from Genoa. In 1802 he designed a hydraulic machine to refine the cocoa paste and mix it with sugar and vanilla. At first, the main competition came from the Swiss chocolate maker Cailler.

The process was progressively perfected and around 1847 the company of Fry and Sons in England introduced a bar of eating chocolate which was a mixture of chocolate and liquor, sugar and cocoa butter. Fry was one of three great Quaker families to go into the chocolate business in England. The other two were the Cadburys and the Rowntrees. John Cadbury had started out selling tea and coffee in Birmingham, and then decided to include chocolate as well. In the beginning he roasted the chocolate beans himself and ground them on his premises. The Rowntree company under another name had been selling chocolate since 1785. Because of their humanitarian tradition, all three families grew concerned about the use of slaves in Portuguese colonies that supplied them with chocolate. They tried to persuade the Portuguese government to end the use of slaves in these colonies, but ultimately were unsuccessful and were forced to take their business elsewhere.

In America, the chocolate industry was started by a doctor and an Irish chocolate maker in 1765. Dr James Baker and John Hannon set up shop in the Massachusetts Bay Colony even before the revolution and sold chocolate with a money-back guarantee. Eventually the company became Baker's Chocolate, still famous today for their blocks of unsweetened baking chocolate. But the company that everyone thinks of when they think of American chocolate is Hershey. Milton Hershey built his first factory in 1903 and ended up with not just chocolate but with a whole town, Hershey, Pennsylvania, and a utopian dream to go with

it. His most famous product was the Hershey bar, a milk chocolate bar in a dark, chocolate-brown wrapper. Hershey's dream was to use mass production to make the Hershey bar cheap enough for every man, woman and child.

Honour for the Swiss

What happened to the Swiss? Although they were the last to enter the chocolate business, they ended up being first among chocolate makers. This happened in part because of the success of the Piedmont factories. Chocolate-making schools were set up there and one young man who did his apprenticeship in Turin returned to Switzerland ready to take on the world. He was François Louis Cailler who in 1819 set up his first chocolate factory near Vevey. This means that the famous Swiss chocolate has only been around for a century and a half.

The Swiss were successful in perfecting the industrial manufacturing of chocolate and the most important result was the invention of milk chocolate around 1875. This was the work of Daniel Peter, who took advantage of a product, powdered milk, made by Henri Nestlé. Peter, who had married one of the Cailler daughters, was also a brilliant businessman and this explains how in 1929 a colossal industry was born that started with the companies of Nestlé, Cailler and another important chocolate manufacturer, Kholer. The conquest of the world chocolate market and related confections was done on a grand scale and the Swiss became chocolate manufacturers *par excellence.* This does not mean, however, that there are not very fine German, Belgian and Dutch chocolate makers.

In fact, one very important improvement in the quality of chocolate was made in 1828 by a Dutchman, Conrad van Hauten who invented a special press to grind the crushed cocoa beans. By doing this he managed to separate the cocoa powder from the butter, so that the former could then be mixed more easily with water and flavourings. He also eliminated chocolate's acidity which tended to give it an unpleasant bitter taste.

Meanwhile, the cultivation of cacao was spreading to new countries: first to Ghana, Nigeria, the Ivory Coast and Cameroon and later reaching Java and New Guinea from the Philippines.

In the earlier part of this century, cocoa and chocolate were advertised and sold as healthy energy-giving foods, especially good for children, adolescents and the physically weak. Cocoa mixed with milk was served as a drink in the morning and as an afternoon snack. As for chocolate, although it was no longer prohibitively expensive, it was still beyond the means of many purses and a box of chocolates was still an irrefutable sign of luxury, of celebration and of privilege. And so it continued to be, at least up to the middle of this century.

From Ersatz Chocolate to Prepared Creams

In Italy during the Second World War somethiing revolutionary happened for the consumer – the manufacture of ersatz chocolate. The idea was for people to feel as if they were not giving up the delicacy, even though there was a war on. So, as the price of cocoa was out of reach, they tried to imitate it. How did they do this? By roasting hazelnuts and making a paste with them, then mixing it with sugar, cocoa powder and vegetable fats. In reality, the result was not at all like the real thing, but it temporarily satisfied mouths made hungry by rationing and sacrifice. When the American soldiers came, bringing nylons, tins of corned beef, and news of a new world to come, they also brought exquisite and highly sought-after chocolate bars from the US army.

In the fifties a product was discovered that used defatted cocoa which was much more economical, still tasted good and was perfect for spreading. Soon, the market was flooded with creams and sweets made with this product which was cheap and perfect for snacks, breakfasts and other refreshments. And it is still adored today by children everywhere.

CHAPTER IV

FROM TREE TO PASTE

As long as the sun
Keeps shining for me,
Oh tree of trees, you will be,
My tonic and the height
Of my truest feelings.

Lorenzo Brancaccio, c1660

A THIN, elegant trunk, with a decorative foliage that changes from red to brown to bronze before turning the dark green of maturity: this is the precious cacao tree, the *cacahuaquahitl* of the Mayas and Aztecs. It reaches a height of more than 35ft/10m in the wild but it is pruned to 15–20ft/5–6m under cultivation on the plantations, to make it easier to harvest. It grows best in the tropics at an altitude of 1,300ft/400m. The best growing conditions require a soil rich in nitrogen and potassium in a humid climate with a temperature range of 68–85°F/20–30°C.

The cacao is a delicate tree that does not tolerate sudden changes of temperature nor does it do well in direct sunlight. Because of this it needs a covering, usually a canopy of trees, to protect it from sun, wind and heavy rains. The cacao is particularly vulnerable when the seeds are planted so a hardier tree such as the banana is generally planted next to each seedling, to act as protection as it grows.

Harvesting the Cocoa Bean

Buds, flowers, leaves and fruit can all be found on the cacao tree simultaneously. It is continuously in flower and new leaves are constantly developing, sprouting directly from the trunk and the thickest branches. Small, yellow or pink flowers, monoclinous, and with no scent, blossom in the third year of growth; most of them fall before they can be pollinated by insects.

Of every hundred blossoms, normally only one develops into fruit over a period of five months. The fruit is an oval-shaped pod pointed on both ends which grow from branches or directly from the trunk. About 6–8 inches/15–20 centimetres long, this seed pod can be as tough as leather when dry. Each pod contains up to forty beans, also called berries, which are arranged in five rows and embedded in a sticky, sweet, white pulp. The beans are made up of a capsule-shaped kernel with two cotyledons and a bean encased in a tannin-rich covering. The pods grow all year round so harvesting can take place at any time, but it is usually done only twice a year. There is a major harvest when the fruit is at its best and a second one when the fruit is of a slightly lower quality.

The pods are ready when they change colour from

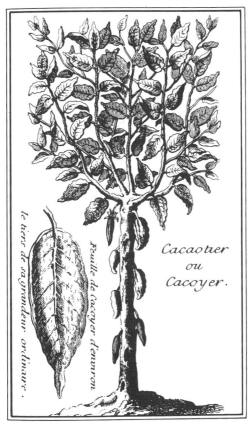

le tiers de sa grandeur ordinaire.

Feuille de Cacoyer d'environ

Cacaotier
ou
Cacoyer.

The cacao tree in a seventeenth-century botanical print

green to yellow, or red to orange, and when they rattle when shaken. From twenty fresh pods about two pounds or one kilo of dried berries are collected. The Brazilian writer Jorge Amado in his novel *Cacao*, set in a *fazenda* where the precious fruit of the cacao tree is harvested and processed, describes some of the high points of the harvest through the eyes of the protagonist: 'The dry leaves of the cacao plant carpet the earth where the snakes warm themselves in the sun after the long rains of June. The fruit hangs from the tree like old lamps. A marvellous mixture of colours that makes everything look beautiful and unreal, except our exhausting work. By seven in the morning we are already removing the beans from the pods, after sharpening our machetes . . .'

The harvester, with a special sickle attached to a pole, cuts the pod, taking care not to damage nearby flowers or buds. The fruit is then cut lengthwise with a machete to release the beans from the pulp.

The beans are put into a tub where they pass through a stage of fermentation, the purpose of which is to eliminate excess pulp and reduce the astringent flavour of the beans. This process also releases the essential oils, which produce the aroma, which will make the end product so valuable.

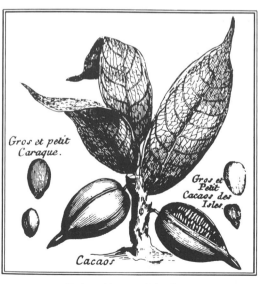

Pods and beans of Theobroma

After almost two weeks, the beans are put on shelves under corrugated iron roofs that protect them from the rain and dried out; once dry, they are put into jute bags and sent across the sea . . . to eagerly awaiting chocolate lovers all over the world.

Which Cacao Tree?

There are three basic varieties of cacao tree: Criollo, Forastero and the hybrids.

The first is the most highly prized but it is also the most delicate and the least productive. Found in Venezuela, Colombia and especially in Mexico, it is originally from the Amazon river area. It has fat, round, light-coloured beans with a sweet flavour that masks a slightly bitter taste. The Forastero, originally from the Upper Amazon and now found in Africa, has more or less flat beans, dark red in colour with thick skins, and a strong, bitter flavour due to a higher tannin content. A robust plant, it grows more quickly than the Criollo and has a higher yield, but the beans are not of such high quality. Once the pluses and minuses of each have been taken into account, many growers plant the two together and develop hybrids from them. The Trinitario for example is a hybrid which combines good qualities from each. There are many other hybrids as well, each with its own flavour, smell and colour. Much like coffee the best chocolate comes from hybrids with a mixture of different qualities, according to formulas which are jealously guarded by each company.

Cocoa Countries

The quality of the beans, as we have seen, varies according to the tree and the country of origin. The variety is reflected in the designation, which frequently includes the name of the area in which it was grown and the port it was shipped from.

Let us look at a list of the principal countries where cocoa is grown and their best-known characteristics.

Central America

Mexico: abundunt production of the varieties based on Criollo and Forastero, many hybrids.

Costa Rica: some good varieties taken from the Trinitario, like Cundeamer and Sangretaro.

Guatemala: average production of very good cocoa with a delicate aroma, either Criollo or Forastero, and a variety of hybrids. Soconusco is highly regarded.

Dominican Republic: the Colabacello is the basic variety, with some Criollo and Forastero. The cocoa is not of particularly high quality because of its somewhat insipid flavour. It is mainly used as an additive to cocoa beans with a stronger flavour.

Jamaica and Grenada: good but limited production, which comes from a selection of Forastero and Trinitario.

South America

Brazil: second largest producer in the world. Forastero is grown most with its varieties, Para Maranhao and Comun. The berry is rich in cocoa butter.

Ecuador: a very aromatic cocoa, among the best in the world, from the strain Forastero Amazonico. The highest quality comes from the Arriba region but greatest production comes from the Esmeralda.

A typical plantation in South America, from an 1876 print

Colombia: abundant production, about 90 per cent of which is from Trinitario Superior.

Venezuela: the most widely grown varieties are Criollo and Colabacello, around Maracaibo and Puerto Cabello, with a low cocoa butter content.

Africa

The cultivation of the cacao plant probably began in the western half of this continent, in Fernando Poo and Santo Tome, through the efforts of Spanish and Portuguese merchants coming from Central and South America between 1870 and 1880. Now this continent produces two-thirds of the world output. It comes mostly from the Forastero plant and is of an average quality which is constantly being improved.

Ivory Coast: this used to be the world leader in production and it continues to be, in terms of quality, the most reliable of the African producers. Of the cocoa grown 95 per cent is of the Forastero strain and the other 5 per cent comes from the Trinitario.

Ghana: the second biggest producer in Africa. The cocoa is of average aroma with a rather bitter flavour.

Nigeria: this country occupies fourth place among world production. Of its cocoa 90 per cent is Forastero.

Santo Tome and Principe: this cocoa is very highly valued among African cocoa because of the high percentage of cocoa butter the beans contain (more than 60 per cent). Various qualities are produced, mostly in Santo Tome which is the larger of the two islands.

Asia

This immense continent has only a limited production of pale cocoa which is not very aromatic.

Sri Lanka: light cocoas, Trinitario, but also Forastero and Amelenado, used most frequently in milk chocolate.

Malaysia: Rapidly becoming one of the main producers in the world; the cocoa has a high acid content but is rich in cocoa butter.

Java and Sumatra: these countries have some of the most beautiful cacao trees, with very dry, light-coloured, large beans, but lacking strong aroma. Used especially for light chocolates (milk chocolate and in chocolate bars).

Oceania

Samoa: aromatic cocoa of great value, derived from Forastero and Criollo hybrids. The Samoan Islands also produce small quantities of a less valuable kind of cocoa. New Guinea: an annual production of 25,000 tons or tonnes of good-quality cocoa.

Shipped from tropical countries to the manufacturers, the sacks of beans are stored in cooled warehouses where they will not absorb odours. The voyage has already been a long one but there are still many processes the beans must go through before they become powder, and even more before they are chocolate bars.

After passing through quality control, the beans are toasted to bring out the cocoa aroma and to help the later separation of the nibs (beans) from the husks. Then they go through a cleaner with a system of brushes and vacuums to eliminate impurities and foreign bodies and prepare them for calibration – the division of beans according to size. Once divided they go on to a final roasting.

The Secret of the Aroma is in the Roasting

That famous, unmistakable enveloping smell which can stimulate our olfactory nerves like few others is completely dependent on this stage, which is crucial to the quality of the finished product. The beans are roasted in huge rotating spheres for fifteen to twenty minutes (depending on the quality of the beans, with higher qualities requiring less time than ordinary ones) at a temperature between 230 and 250°F/110 and 120°C, again depending on quality.

This process removes any dampness and acidity, and encourages the development of the aromatic essences, but only an expert can decide just when the roasting should stop; too long and the beans will char.

After a quick cooling by ventilation, the beans are put into a winnowing machine that removes the husks and crushes the beans. Through a system of descending sieves, the roasted nibs are selected, ground (during which time the cocoa butter is melted) and made into a fluid paste, called chocolate liquor.

The Non-parallel Lives of Chocolate and Hot Cocoa

Both cocoa powder and chocolate have common roots: they both come from the cocoa paste which is dissolved in water, ground very fine and partially defatted through a series of hydraulic presses. Here the cocoa butter surfaces as a yellow oil which can be filtered, passed through several sieves and finally cooled.

What remains is a solid, the very hard 'block' or dry-press cake, which contains 8 to 26 per cent cocoa butter condensed under 600 atmospheres of pressure, and which will be ground to a very fine powder.

To make chocolate, different qualities of non-defatted cocoa pastes are mixed according to special secret formulas that hold the key to their quality.

Various other ingredients are added to the paste to obtain the kind of chocolate desired: cocoa butter, sugar (the proportion of cocoa and sugar is what determines the quality of chocolate, especially with plain chocolate), powdered milk and spices. The paste that results is put into a mixer at a refinery where the different qualities of cocoa are unified according to flavour, colour and aroma. After this treatment, the size of the particles should not measure more than 25 microns.

The Crowning Glory of the Process: the Mixing

I am describing all these processes with an objectivity that the clearly very technical subject seems to require, but I must confess that to go in person to a famous factory and visit the laboratories is an incredible experience. Everything there is done the way it was fifty years ago and longer, and everyone seems to have an enormous pride in their great tradition and an awareness of being exceptional in the safeguarding of their art. In the big factories everything is much more automated, though this does not necessarily mean that the finished product is any worse.

But there in that temple of chocolate, a wood-burning roasting machine is still in operation. Only olive wood is used because it burns with a clean smokeless flame which will not contaminate the cocoa, highly sensitive to odours and flavours. Mad? Perhaps, but the success of these purists is increasing, a tribute to the quality of their product.

Let us return though to our subject, the mixing, which is without doubt the most fascinating phase of the process, since this is when chocolate takes on its individual character. Try to imagine huge metal receptacles as big as bathtubs filled with a semi-liquid, dark paste which is beaten and aerated for hours and hours without interruption at a constant temperature of 140–176°F/60–80°C. Right before your fascinated eyes, it moves and rolls and turns over on itself with a uniform cadence, becoming ever smoother, meanwhile the fragrance that the creamy mass gives off envelops you till you feel quite dizzy.

There is no escaping it: even as it is being slowly prepared for its eventual encounter with the consumer, chocolate has a sensual aggressiveness.

The mixing can go on for hours or even days according to the flavour of chocolate desired. In this the tastes of each country come into play: American chocolate which is rather harsh to a European is mixed for eighteen hours, while Swiss chocolate which is incredibly velvety is mixed for seventy-two hours. Then the temperature of the liquid paste is reduced and very fine crystallization of the cocoa butter takes place. This safeguards the consistency of the product which otherwise might be affected by sudden temperature changes that can occur when it is put into stainless steel moulds to shape it.

When I visited the factory it was close to Easter and there were long tables full of shiny moulds in the shape of half an egg, of all sizes one inside the other, waiting to be covered with a blanket of dark velvety chocolate: a metaphysical vision of what really goes on in chocolate production.

The moulds full of this smooth paste move along a constantly vibrating belt meant to eliminate air bubbles and make the paste adhere to the moulds. Then they cross over to a cooling tunnel with a temperature of 43°F/6°C where the chocolate solidifies and contracts, ready for extraction from the mould.

The last phase is the confectionary stage but this is only reached after another one hundred hours of preparation, each step being done with scrupulous care.

The bars are wrapped in three layers: the innermost layer, aluminum foil, is covered by a greaseproof paper and finally the whole thing is wrapped in a printed coloured outside wrapper. Chocolates (as opposed to bars) can be 'bare' or covered with a layer of aluminium which is sometimes embossed.

A Guide to the Products

As an older man, Voltaire consumed 'twelve cups of chocolate from five in the morning until three in the afternoon'. This was all he ate until then, which was both very sumptuous and very pleasant to the palate. In those days chocolate, which came in solid blocks that were crushed into powder before being used, was only consumed in liquid form. It was dissolved in boiling water with sugar and occasionally spices over a hot flame and then beaten with expert hands. Today's selection is very different, given the many different kinds of tastes and uses. Below we will try to clarify them.

Powders and Pastes

Cocoa powder: pure, bitter cocoa powder, with most of the cocoa butter removed (between 24 and 26 per cent remains), used especially in confectionery.
Sweetened cocoa powder: cocoa powder to which a certain amount of sugar has been added, used in making hot chocolate.
Cocoa paste: cocoa beans reduced to a paste through a mechanical process, with all the natural fats intact.

Bars

In this group there are basic distinctions that the industry makes:

Plain chocolate: this contains cocoa paste, cocoa butter and sugar and is divided further into 'extra' (no less than 45 per cent superior quality cocoa with at least 28 per cent cocoa butter and no more than 55 per cent sugar), 'regular' (no less than 43 per cent cocoa of medium quality with at least 26 per cent cocoa butter and no more than 57 per cent sugar), and 'semisweet' (no less than 35 per cent cocoa of average quality with at least 18 per cent cocoa butter and no more than 65 per cent sugar). There is also German sweet cooking chocolate in America which is similar to 'semisweet' chocolate but which must contain a minimum of 15 per cent pure chocolate.

Unsweetened chocolate is hard to find in the United Kingdom though it is widely used in the United States and known as baking chocolate. It is pure chocolate with no sugar or flavourings added.

Milk chocolate: this is a mixture of cocoa paste, cocoa butter, sugar and milk (concentrated or powdered). Either whole milk or skimmed milk may be used but if skimmed milk is used it must say so plainly on the label.

Milk chocolate is subdivided into two categories, one with no less than 25 per cent cocoa, 3.5 per cent milk fats, and 14 per cent solid milk products and no more than 55 per cent sugar; the other containing less cocoa.

White chocolate: this contains at least 20 per cent cocoa butter, sugar, and powdered milk.

Filled chocolate: there must be a chocolate covering of at least 25 per cent of the total weight with a filling of liqueur, cream, fruit, nuts and so on.

Couverture or covering chocolate: another cocoa-based product used for sweets. It is a fondant or milk chocolate.

CHAPTER V

AN INVITING DRINK

Twill make Old Women Young and Fresh,
Create New Motions of the Flesh,
And cause them to long for you know what,
If they but taste of Chocolate.

James Wadsworth,
The Nature and Quality of Chocolate

DARK and thick, hot and velvety, fragrant and voluptuous, hot chocolate has its own season. It begins with the first chill of autumn and lasts until the final cold days of winter. When clouds and dampness envelop us and the wind nips our fingers and nose, it is time to turn to hot chocolate for help. Nothing else can comfort, console and strengthen us like it can, nothing can revive flagging spirits and infuse us with such a feeling of wellbeing, and a sense that all is right with the world. 'It is like my mother,' someone once said, 'It is affectionate and warm and loving and it leaves me feeling happy and content.'

A drink to enjoy alone if we are feeling self-indulgent and to sip in company if, on the contrary, we feel like chatting and baring our souls. A traditional drink for women meeting in tearooms and cafés, it is the ideal hot drink for lovers. Since we generally drink it with a certain dark sense of guilt (it's fattening, it gives you spots) we should serve it with a sense of ritual so we are not disappointed. Unfortunately, the drink that cafés and snack bars serve today is mostly mass produced and colourless, though one can still find the occasional delicious exception.

The delightful 'Chocolate Drinker', an engraving taken from the picture of the same name by François de Troy

From Pot to Cup

For hot chocolate to offer all the delight it is capable of providing it must be served properly. The ideal way would be to make it in a pot first and then serve it in cups.

In the old days, both the utensil the chocolate was made in and the receptacle it was served in were called chocolate pots. The first had to be fire-resistant and was often made of copper coated with tin. Since preparation required it to come to a full boil and be stirred constantly, a tall pot was used with an opening left in the top for the handle of the whisk used to stir the mixture of cocoa and milk or cocoa and water.

The chocolate pot that was part of the dinner service, usually of porcelain or silver, had similar characteristics. Generally the top was perforated and had a knob to make it easier to open. The upper part of the pot had a long wooden handle sticking out at a right angle. To keep it stable as its contents boiled, it was often placed on a three-legged stand under which an alcohol brazier was kept burning to keep it hot afterwards.

Today it is very difficult to find such a pot. Collectors and antique dealers say that although there are many tea and coffee pots around, to come across a chocolate pot is quite rare. In the eighteenth century, coffee pots with lids, especially those made of porcelain, were used indiscriminately for all three exotic drinks, tea, coffee and chocolate. Afterwards, chocolate had its own receptacle and, as always happens, people competed for the most beautiful and most original. In 1691, the Parisian paper *Le livre commode* announced that there were 'portable chocolate pots that fit in a handbag' which included a brazier, alcohol, matches, cups, saucers and spoons as well as the chocolate and sugar necesary 'for three drinks'.

There were also exquisite chocolate pots made of gold, according to an inventory of the goods of the Crown made in April 1697. Today, even in the most elaborate services, a chocolate pot is not included though there is still a tea pot or coffee pot.

A pretty porcelain cup with a somewhat narrow but ample shape will hold the chocolate elegantly. Interestingly enough, tall glass-shaped cups without handles

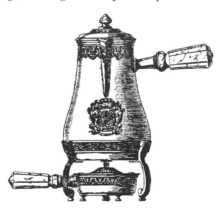

were manufactured as chocolate cups in Meissen, the famous German capital of porcelain, around 1740 and chocolate cups with two handles and sometimes with lids to keep the chocolate hot were also made. Another type of cup with a small saucer was very popular in Vienna around 1720. It was called a 'trombleuse' and was shaped like a glass but it was fortified with an inner rim around the centre of the plate to make it more stable.

Manual Dexterity

To prepare chocolate, one tool which we have already mentioned was essential: the whisk. A wooden beater similar to the ones used to get rid of bubbles in sparkling wines and champagne, it beat the cocoa drink, blending it and making it velvety and foamy.

The thickest part of the chocolate tends to settle at the bottom and in fact there was a popular Venetian saying, 'coffee at the head, chocolate at the tail' which means, more or less, that the best coffee is the part at the top of the pot (while the grounds settle to the bottom), while with chocolate the best part falls to the bottom (because it is the heaviest). This saying is still true, even though people do not usually serve chocolate any more by rhythmically beating it with a whisk. Sometimes though one can still find tearooms or cafés where young waiters are given this job.

One such servant, as uninhibited in life as in love, appears in Mozart's comic opera, *Cosi fan tutte* (1790). While she prepares the drink, Despina cannot help but complain of the life she leads, constantly at the service of others:

. . . We run from morning to night,
They afflict us, they use us . . .
I have been waiting for an hour with breakfast ready,
And all I can enjoy of the chocolate is its smell.
Isn't it as good for me as it is for my mistresses?
Of course it is, pretty ladies,
You get to drink it, while all I get to do is look.
Well, all right . . . I want to taste it:
How delicious!

Sweet Initiation

A voluptuous aphrodisiac, a favourite of the gods: for me, hot chocolate will always be linked with childhood.

Then it meant a treat, a party and it was also part of the investitures, the ritual passages in one's childhood. In my house, first communion was followed by a family reception where all our friends and cousins and schoolmates gathered around a huge table. If I close my eyes I can still see the tablecloth from Flanders and the little lace mats on silver plates filled with pastries and *beignets*, the flowered porcelain cups, the chairs round the table with cushions for the little ones and at the head of the table, the place of honour, recognizable because it had the exquisite gold and white cup, that had been religiously passed down from generation to generation and into which boiling chocolate was poured, thick, foamy and light, flowing languidly and with great promise from

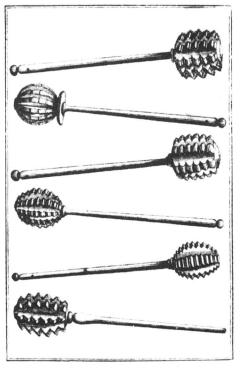

Various whisks used to beat the chocolate, from a drawing done in 1687

the mouth of the pot with the decorated lid. Years later, I read that Gertrude in *The Betrothed* by Alessandro Manzoni drank chocolate too and this drink marked a fundamental passage to adulthood for her and was part of the rite of initiation.

When the young girl in the book, giving up her own interests, finally submits to paternal wishes, and agrees to take the veil, it happens like this: 'She dressed quickly, had her hair combed and appeared in the drawing room where her parents and brother were. They made her sit down in an armchair and brought her a cup of hot chocolate, which in those days was the same as being given the *toga virilis* among the ancient Romans.'

For today's children, there is no particular ritual attached to drinking hot chocolate. Accustomed as they are to eating peanut butter and marmite from jars, to having snacks of chocolate drink from the refrigerator or the local food shop at any hour of the day, chocolate has no emotional associations. But one day you should try making it the old-fashioned, authentic, way, hot and fragrant, for a birthday party for example, and serve it instead of coca cola, even if it takes more time to prepare and it gets chocolate stains all over your tablecloth and even if after all your efforts someone still asks for 'a coke'.

If you have doubts about the effort involved, consider that wonderful smell that reaches right into your heart. Enjoy the secret pleasure of the genuine gourmand, leaving some bits in the pan after dissolving the chocolate so that later you can go back and lick them off your spoon when no one is looking.

There are many recipes for making a good cup of hot chocolate. But do not confuse hot chocolate with cocoa. The first is made with real chocolate, the second with cocoa powder and the difference is enormous. The following are some recipes, offered with just one piece of advice: always use ingredients of the highest quality and if you aspire to perfection, follow the rules I give you here which I received from experts.

You will see just how easy it is to make a delicious drink and how happy you will make the ones who will savour it.

The Art of Preparing Chocolate

Anyone who thinks that all it takes to melt chocolate is to put it in a pan over a hot flame and wait until it dissolves is mistaken. Chocolate requires attentive, loving care; left to itself, it may take revenge by burning.

To avoid catastrophes, here are some ways to melt chocolate that I have learned from experience:

Using steam: fill a pot with hot water and put it over the fire, but do not let it boil. Place the chocolate you want to melt in a slightly smaller pan that will fit into the first (a double-boiler is perfect). If you are melting a very small amount, you can even put the chocolate into a cup.

In the oven: put the chocolate into a heat-resistant dish, like a pyrex one, and then into a warm but not hot oven and turn off the oven. Check it often as it melts.

On top of the stove: this is the trickiest method. Put the chocolate into a thick-bottomed saucepan over a very low heat and stir it constantly. Take it off the heat as soon as it begins to dissolve.

A good rule for all these methods is to take the chocolate from the heat as soon as it begins to melt because it will contine to melt away from the heat; keep stirring it until it is fluid and well mixed. Some other tips are:

- To save time, grate the chocolate first, especially if it is a small amount.

- Milk chocolate should be dissolved more slowly than other kinds.

- Dark chocolate when it melts, liquefies, while sweet, semi-sweet and milk chocolate tend to keep their original shape unless you mix them.

- Once dissolved, different types of chocolate have different consistencies: bitter is the most fluid, while milk chocolate is the most dense.

- The utensils used to melt chocolate for hot chocolate must be perfectly dry because a single drop of water is enough to thicken and make lumpy what should be fluid and creamy. If it does happen, however, there is a remedy: add a little solid vegetable fat. Butter is not good because it contains water and, for the same reason, do not add water itself. The proportions are one teaspoonful for every ounce/28 grams of chocolate; mix it with care after the chocolate is melted.

English Chocolate

For four/five servings: prepare tea with sugar for four servings. Dissolve four teaspoonsful of cocoa in three cups of milk (adding it little by little) and add seven teaspoonsful of sugar. Mix the cocoa and tea together and serve the drink in big glasses with one or two ice cubes.

Hot Chocolate

For two servings: you will need a medium-sized bar of plain chocolate and 1 pint/½ litre of milk. Preparation is simple: put the milk in a pan with the chocolate, broken into chunks, and heat, stirring from time to time, until it is thick. If you like a thicker chocolate, you can add some cornflour dissolved in a little cold water.

Brazilian Hot Chocolate

For four servings: melt several teaspoonsful of cocoa powder in half a cup of hot, strong coffee and heat the mixture until it boils. Add three cups of boiling milk and mix vigorously. Leave the drink in a bain-marie for ten minutes and serve it in cups, adding whipped cream if you like.

Swiss Hot Chocolate

For one serving: melt a teaspoonful of cocoa powder in half a cup of milk. When the mixture is well blended, add another half-cup of milk. Add a teaspoonful of cream and stir well before serving.

Fragrant Hot Chocolate

Melt a medium-sized bar of plain chocolate with a little milk, then add more milk, a drop of vanilla, a sprinkling of cinnamon, a tiny piece of lemon peel and sugar to taste. Separately, dissolve a pinch of cornflour in a little milk and add it to the chocolate. Bring the mixture to the boil twice and serve very hot.

Syracuse Chocolate

You will need a medium-sized bar of plain chocolate, two teaspoonsful of condensed milk, four tablespoons of orange juice, two teaspoonsful of brandy and two teaspoonsful of gin. Put the chocolate over the fire with half a cup of water and the condensed milk. Stir until it is a thin cream and then add the brandy and gin. When the mixture has cooled, add the orange juice. Mix well and refrigerate. Serve cold with ice cubes.

Barbajada

This is a famous old Milanese drink, invented it is said by a theatrical empresario named Barbaja. The recipe is not complicated. You will need three small cups of hot chocolate made with water and cocoa powder, three small cups of milk and three small cups of espresso coffee. In a round copper bowl, put the chocolate, coffee and milk. Place the bowl over heat and beat the contents constantly. When a white foam forms around the surface, pour the 'barbajada' into a cup and serve immediately. In summer, the drink is best served cold.

Perfect Company

What is the best thing to serve with hot chocolate?

In the morning, rolls, croissants, buttered toast, and sweet rolls all are good. As an afternoon snack or for tea, most pastries and sweets go well with it.

For those with more of a sweet tooth, the ultimate is to top off hot chocolate with a big cloud of whipped cream, which should be served separately in a little crystal glass and delicately spooned on the hot chocolate in the presence of the guest. Nor should you omit a large sugar bowl for those guests who feel that the drink, although perfect for some palates, is not sufficiently sweet for them. For the benefit of your guests, always have the chocolate ready when they arrive. You can keep it hot in a bain-marie; all you then need to do is to beat it just before serving.

Our predecessors, in fact, were aware that day-old chocolate was even better than freshly prepared because it was more concentrated.

Here is a bit of advice from one Madame d'Austel, the mother superior of the Convent of the Visitation in Belley, Italy, in the nineteenth century: make your hot chocolate in a ceramic coffee pot the day before, let it rest and do not worry about it. The nun went on to point out, with a candour which suggests a certain sense of guilt, that 'God will not be offended by this small refinement since He Himself is perfection'.

CHAPTER VI

THE ART OF CONFECTIONERY, CAKES AND DESSERTS

. . . they offered us a light, fleeting chocolate cream . . .

Marcel Proust, Swann's Way *(1913)*

WHAT would the art of confectionery be if chocolate did not exist? It is better not to think such a sad thought, since so many exquisite things, in the shape of tarts, creams, icecreams, pastries and fondants, come from the confectioner's kitchen, and end up triumphantly in shop windows, making our lives happier, by charmingly finishing off a meal to the applause of guests.

Great Britain has traditionally turned to fruits and spices when preparing sweet dishes, a reflection perhaps

of her own colonies in the East and her excellent fresh fruit. Typical British desserts are fruit pies and puddings, spicy teacakes and breads. But Eliza Acton, the nineteenth-century cookery writer, offered recipes both for chocolate custard and for chocolate drops and today British cooks can find plenty of recipes for chocolate cakes and biscuits as cookery writers find inspiration from abroad.

America on the other hand is mad about chocolate desserts. Some of the classic ones are the famous brownie, made with unsweetened chocolate, eggs, butter and sugar, chocolate chip cookies, so successful now that they are sold all over in specialized stores, fudge (which is also made all over Britain), chocolate cheesecake and chocolate cream pie. And, of course, every family has its treasured recipe for chocolate cake. Two favourites are devil's food cake, made with cocoa powder which gives it a reddish tint, and German chocolate cake.

Speaking of chocolate cakes, let us not forget to mention the indisputable masterpiece of its kind, the famous sachertorte, Viennese in origin but known throughout the world and widely imitated.

An Ode to Chocolate 'Tortes'

The year is 1832. Prince Klemens Wenzel Lothar Metternich-Winneburg, Chancellor and Minister of Foreign Affairs of the Austrian Empire, asks his cook to prepare a dessert that is 'thick, compact and masculine'.

The cook, Eduard Sacher, makes several attempts and finally comes up with his masterpiece, the sachertorte. Afterwards, he opens a hotel which becomes the most famous in Vienna and where naturally this sublime pastry is served.

But the best-known pastry shop in Vienna, Demel, also had its version of the sachertorte. The difference lay in the marmalade, which was always apricot. In the Demel 'torte', with only one layer, it was on top, just under the layer of chocolate, while in the sachertorte, which had two layers, it was in the middle between them. The dispute between the two *maîtres-pâtissiers* to determine who was the owner of the true recipe was inevitable and it ended up in court, dragging on for seven years.

In the end the Hotel Sacher won, and its creation was given the seal of authenticity. (Demel, for his part, had revenge later by winning the right to call his own 'the original Sachertorte'.)

There are many recipes in circulation for this dessert with its compact layer of dark chocolate pastry, thin, dry and not very sweet, the perfect combination in its studied simplicity of what could almost be defined as the essence of a chocolate 'torte'. If you go through cookery books, you will not find two recipes alike for sacher (the original recipe is still a secret). However, I offer you one below that is very reliable.

Before we go to the kitchen to try some of these chocolate desserts, I think it would be useful first to make some general observations on the confectionary traditions that have developed on the two sides of the ocean. This seems appropriate given the increasing number of links and exchanges between the Old World and the New and because of the many books with recipes using chocolate published so successfully in the United States.

Two Points of View on Chocolate

The European tradition is generally linked to an elegant sobriety and understatement: tarts, usually of only one layer, are usually not very sweet. They melt in the mouth smoothly, subtly and moistly and there is no more than just a hint of fine, delicate chocolate, completely without ostentation (notable exceptions are the Hungarian dobostort and the rigojanczi with seven and even eight layers and the sumptuous central European creations in which chocolate, whipped cream and cherries all triumph). A famous American cook, aware of the fascination the Old World holds, confessed: 'For me, there is nothing like a delicate chocolate tart with a fine dark covering; it is sort of the edible equivalent of the little black dress that never goes out of style in a woman's wardrobe.'

American sweets on the other hand, even though excellent, are often somewhat parvenu: devil's food cake and angel food cake with three, five, even eight layers held together by rich cream fillings full of calories, disappear under deluges of thick chocolate and the whole thing is topped with dollops of whipped cream. Some even have names which are numbers: mile high icecream pie, for example, is a pie filled with chocolate cream topped with a cover of meringue four inches high and this is topped with chocolate sauce. Even brownies, those famous American cake-like desserts are just used as a base for a scoop of vanilla icecream which is then followed with chocolate fudge sauce and on top, a big dollop of whipped cream. Caught in the whirl of an insane passion, Americans still cannot avoid a sense of guilt that their puritan roots impose on them for abandoning themselves to this delicious vice. In an effort to exorcize it they have named their downfalls 'chocolate sins', 'chocolate decadence', 'mort au chocolat' (a true *cupio dissolvi* with chocolate present in every part of it, from the meringue to the sponge cake to the cream to the mousse). In this way, their morals have been protected; those who persevere, swallowing without heed, have been warned.

However, temptations continue, especially among the traditionally more conservative Europeans who have begun to be influenced by American creativity. What start out as brilliantly simple ideas, like strawberries dipped in chocolate, and chocolate *fondue* in which pineapple, bananas, mandarin oranges, dates, cherries, dried apricots and whatever strikes your fancy are all dipped, go on to become sur-realist creations. You can now find little bags made of chocolate and fancifully filled with coloured fruit creams, or incredible cabbage tarts that have only their shape in common with the real thing, and giant chocolate roses, whose petals are for picking and eating.

Ten Reliable Recipes

One should always have cocoa (sweet or dark, but always of the finest quality) and chocolate blocks on hand in the kitchen, ready to be put to use in making cakes, puddings, sauces and tarts.

Traditional or new, simple or elaborate, recipes are a constant challenge to one's creativity and talents as a cook. I have chosen a few of my favourites for you. *Bon appetit!*

Hazelnuts with Chocolate

The ideal accompaniment for afternoon tea, but also just the thing to offer guests after a meal. I must confess I am selfish, and once I get started eating these, it is rare that there are any left for others.

7oz/200g shelled hazelnuts, 7oz/200g plain chocolate, grated, sugar, a small glass brandy or other sweet liqueur
Toast the nuts in the oven, then remove the dark peel and chop them very fine. Mix with the grated chocolate and add liqueur to taste, stirring until you get a well-mixed paste of medium consistency. If necessary, add a little cold milk. Form the mixutre into small balls about the size of a hazelnut, roll them in the sugar until they are completely covered and put them on greaseproof paper or in little paper baking cups.

Chocolate Cream

Oh, delight, delight of my heart! A supreme dessert for an elegant lunch or dinner.

7oz/200g plain chocolate, 7oz/200g sugar, 4 egg yolks, vanilla pod, 1¼ pints/¾ litre cream, 2oz/50g flaked chocolate, 8 amaretto (macaroon) biscuits, some sweet liqueur (orange, cognac, rum)

Grate the chocolate. Over a low heat, warm two-thirds of the cream with the sugar and vanilla pod until the sugar dissolves. Separately beat the egg yolks in a bowl and slowly add the cream and sugar mixture. Melt the chocolate in a double saucepan, add it to the eggs and cream, then heat this mixture in the double saucepan, stirring over a low heat till it thickens. Remove it from the heat and add a few drops of liqueur for flavouring, and leave to cool. Put two amaretto biscuits soaked in a little liqueur in each bowl, pour the chocolate cream over them and place in the refrigerator. When ready to serve, whip the remaining cream and decorate each bowl with cream and chocolate flakes.

Chocolate Sauce

Good for hundreds of occasions, this very easy preparation goes beautifully with vanilla icecream or over a rather bland homemade cake to give it more flavour.

5oz/150g plain chocolate, ½ teasp vanilla essence, 3tbsp cream, ½oz/15g butter

Dissolve the chocolate in 7floz/200ml water, add the vanilla essence and let the mixture cook over a low heat for fifteen minutes, stirring constantly. Away from the heat, add the three tablespoons of cream and the butter. Serve in a sauce bowl.

Chocolate Soufflé

Another marvellous dessert, pretty to look at, pretty to sink a spoon in. The only danger, as with all soufflés, is that it does not rise and thus does not arrive at the table proud and puffed up.

2tbsp flour, 4oz/100g sugar, 2oz/40g butter, 5 eggs, 1 cup milk, 4oz/100g dark cocoa powder, unsweetened, half a vanilla pod, icing sugar

Heat oven to 375°F/190°C/mark 5. Butter a soufflé dish.
Bring the milk to the boil with the half vanilla pod, then melt the butter in a saucepan, add the flour, stirring it in, then the boiling milk and let this cook for ten minutes, stirring constantly as if you were making a white sauce. Remove from the heat, add the sugar and the egg yolks and beat with a whisk until a creamy, well-blended, thick mixture. Add the cocoa, and continue stirring. Beat the egg whites till stiff and carefully incorporate them into the mixture. Pour it into the soufflé dish and put this into the hot oven. Check after twenty minutes and cook the soufflé until it is well puffed up. Then remove it, sprinkle the top with powdered sugar and serve.

Almost Sachertorte

5oz/150g plain chocolate, 3½oz/100g butter, 5oz/150g flour, 5oz/150g sugar, 6 eggs, separated, gelatine, apricot jam

Grate the chocolate and let it melt over a very low heat,

adding the previously melted butter and mixing carefully. Separately beat the egg yolks with the sugar until they are light and fluffy, then add the chocolate and butter. Let this cool. Beat the egg whites until stiff, sprinkle the flour over them, folding it in, and carefully add this to the chocolate mixture. Preheat the oven to 350°F/180°C/mark 4. Put the mixture into a buttered baking tin and bake for forty minutes.

Let the torte cool, then unmould it and cut it horizontally into two layers. Put apricot jam or apricot jelly between the layers. Note: the torte should not be more than about one inch/two centimetres high.

Finish it with a thin coating of chocolate made by melting 2oz/50g plain chocolate with three tablespoons of water. Away from the heat, add 7oz/200g icing sugar to the chocolate and water and work the mixture until it is smooth and well blended. Let it rest a few hours and coat the sides and top of the cake.

Chocolate Walnut Tart

This is a dessert I often make at home and have served goodness knows how many times, always very successfully.

5oz/140g plain chocolate, 5oz/140g shelled walnuts, 5oz/140g sugar, 4 eggs, separated, 2oz/50g candied peel

Crush slightly the peeled walnuts with some of the sugar. Beat the egg yolks with the remaining sugar, add the grated chocolate, then the beaten egg whites and the candied peel cut into small pieces. Put the mixture into a greased baking dish and let it cook in a moderate oven (350°F/180°C/mark 4) for about forty minutes.

Chocolate Shake

7oz/200g plain chocolate, 1 pint/½litre milk, 14 fl oz/ 400ml cream, 6 tbsp sugar, 4 tbsp crushed ice

Grate the chocolate and dissolve it in a double saucepan over a low heat. Add the milk, cream, sugar and crushed ice. Put all this in a liquidizer and liquidize until creamy. Serve in tall glasses.

This velvety drink can be served with a meal or as an indulgent snack on a summer's day along with thin biscuits or little pastries.

Chocolate Mousse

12oz/350g plain chocolate, 2oz/50g butter, 3 egg yolks, 4 egg whites, 4½oz/125g sugar

In a bowl, cream the egg yolks and sugar until they are smooth and creamy. If you have a liquidizer or food processor, it only takes a minute. Break up the chocolate and melt it in a double saucepan.

Away from the heat, add the softened butter and then add the beaten egg yolks. Mix well and carefully add the stiffly beaten egg whites. Place in a mould or in individual cups and let cool in the refrigerator for at least three hours.

I highly recommend this sweet, aphrodisiac because of its creamy, velvety consistency. It is the perfect finish to an intimate dinner.

Chocolate Nougat

9oz/250g butter, 7oz/200g plain sweet biscuits, 4 egg yolks, 5oz/150g cocoa powder, 4oz/100g toasted almonds, 2oz/50g toasted hazelnuts, 2oz/50g candied peel, 2oz/50g raisins, 2oz/50g pinenuts

In a bowl, beat the egg yolks and butter. Add the cocoa powder, a little at a time, then the crumbled biscuits, the almonds, the hazelnuts, the pinenuts, the chopped candied peel and the raisins. Mix together and put into a rectangular mould, lined with greaseproof paper. Bang the mould against a hard surface a few times so the mixture is uniform, then put it into the refrigerator for a few hours. To serve, remove from the mould and cut into slices.

CHAPTER VII

THE ARDENT, SEDUCTIVE SOLID

I'd make a thousand trips
to his lips
if I were a bee,
because he's sweeter than
chocolate candy to me.

From a song by Billie Holliday

HOT chocolate is a pleasure we allow ourselves from time to time when we feel like being self indulgent. But we usually enjoy a bar of chocolate, or a sweet much more often – in fact, whenever the urge strikes us. Bars of chocolate are so much easier to obtain, there's nothing to make, and they are so nice to offer to other people and to give as gifts.

Chocolate is a double pleasure: when it comes in the form of hot chocolate in a cup you can savour it slowly, letting it trickle slowly down your throat, so it spreads its smooth heat to the most intimate fibres of your body; when it is in solid form, you can enjoy the more concrete pleasure of chewing it, you can feel it dissolve, become liquid in your mouth, melting, cheering you like nothing else. In fact, if in relation to coffee and tea, hot chocolate has had a less brilliant destiny, in its solid form it has enjoyed incredible success, becoming the quintessence of exquisiteness, both symbol and myth for the temptations of gluttony.

Let's take a closer look at the secrets of solid chocolate, a fascinating subject which has not yet been studied exhaustively.

Among the many manuals and treatises that have appeared in recent years on the subject of chocolate, none of them has considered bars of chocolate because the books cater for the do-it-yourself approach, offering recipes and preparations made by hand. This is a serious omission so far as authentic chocophiles are concerned as they do not necessarily want to make this heavenly

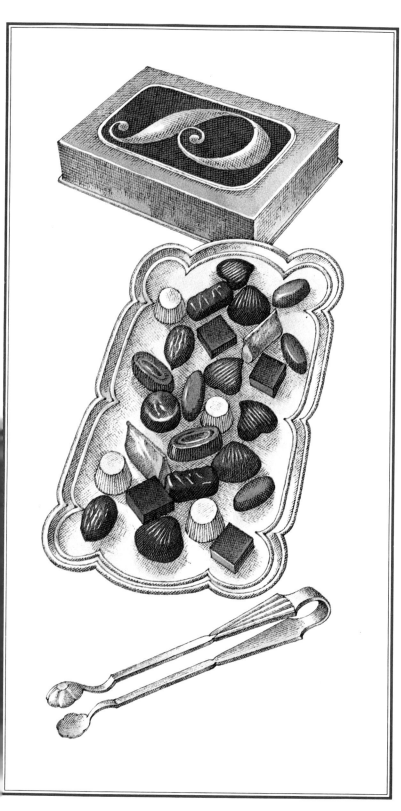

delicacy themselves, but are nevertheless faithful consumers of the products of the art of chocolate making.

Dark or Milk Chocolate?

This is a fundamental distinction that divides chocolate lovers into two camps. The connoisseurs – there is no point in hiding it – clearly prefer dark chocolate. For them, it is chocolate *par excellence*, dark and virile. Made for carnivores, it should be sniffed first, like a fine wine, to savour its full chocolaty aroma and then eaten in small bites to enjoy fully the pleasure, letting it melt with inexpressible languor on the palate and tongue.

As for milk chocolate, the judgement of the connoisseur is slightly prejudiced; it is too sweet, too smooth, it is best for children they say, as if this preference implied a state of gustatory immaturity, of childish tastebuds perpetually in search of sweets.

But it is a matter of scarce importance for the great mass of chocolate addicts who equitably divide their loyalties between dark and milk, in all their infinite varieties and adorned with every filling imaginable, satisfying even the wildest fantasies.

A Bar of Chocolate equals Perfect Happiness

Shaped into a flat rectangle, or in its classic form, divided into small squares to make it easier to break, wrapped in foil to keep it intact and fragrant, and then wrapped again in coloured paper printed with its brand, weight, ingredients and other seductions.

There it is, the bar of chocolate, ready and full of promise. A good part of its fascination lies in its geometric shape, in its squareness, but everything about it is charming: sometimes we see almonds or hazelnuts poking out of its smooth surface, at other times it is the creamy filling or a liqueur filling advertised on its wrapper that tempts us, or it's marzipan, or a crunchy filling or lemon peel, or perhaps it's an orange filling or bits of coconut encased in a fine, hard layer of chocolate, creating a secure container for its variegated delights.

The bar of chocolate is a geometric temptation, a rectangular call that is hard to resist. For someone who loves chocolate it is almost impossible to start a bar of chocolate without finishing it. Along with its traditional shape, which can be any size from small to gigantic, there is also the big solid block of chocolate, little chocolate drops, and the ingot-shaped bar, not to mention all the different shapes that abandon geometry completely and turn up as hearts, cigarettes, pieces of fruit and even giant sweets.

The precursor of the chocolate bar seems to have been made by the Florentine, Carletti, who 'found the way to add citrus peel and lemon peel and the very pleasant odour of jasmine'. So say the chronicles, at least. Chocolate scented with bits of candied citrus fruit was also Italian. Later the French courts brought it to perfection.

This was where another delicacy, praline, was born, taking its name from the duke of Plessis-Praslin, whose kitchens developed it. It happened that a young *pâtissier* in a moment of carelessness let some caramelized sugar fall into a bowl of almonds. Not having enough time to do anything about this he took the stuff to the table covered with a chocolate sauce to hide his mistake. The combination of flavours so pleased the duke that he declared it a new dessert and modestly named it after himself, declaring it a discovery for the pleasure of humanity.

The direct predecessor of the modern bar of chocolate and chocolates was documented in 1720 in the words of a certain abbot Labat (yet another religious person in the history of chocolate) who, writing about a trip made to Martinique, said, 'chocolate is used to make big bars, little bars called "diablotins" [from the devil, another oft-repeated idea] and a kind of marmalade in which they put candied pinenuts'.

But, as we have seen, the bar of chocolate did not become widespread for another century. At first it was prepared and handed out as an afternoon snack in religious communities: simple, and not too expensive, it could be eaten with bread, it was filling and was easily served. But it was still considered a poor cousin to hot chocolate. The first to appreciate it truly were the Swiss who sensed its many possibilities and thought up all kinds of capricious fillings and shapes.

They formed the bars using metal moulds with tin linings; today most moulds are plastic. The surface traditionally is divided into smaller squares of chocolate and, according to experts, this is not only because they are easier to break but because this kind of design also hides imperfections, the unattractive wrinkles and cracks that can ruin the delicate surface.

The wrapper, formerly of very fine tin, is made today of less expensive aluminium, with a silvery inside and an outside that is often printed and in colour. The kind and quality of the wrapper is often a good indication of the quality of the chocolate, so, beware the trappings!

The Olympics of Chocolates

Chocolates, 'bite-size products' as they are defined by law, are sold either by the piece or in a box and are truly one of life's pleasures; they are perhaps one of the smallest and most traditional treasures to be within reach of any purse or palate. Their names, which vary according to their ingredients and shape, historical or pure invention, have by now entered into the annals of the chocolate-making tradition, but there are still hundreds of them since each manufacturer baptizes their own products.

For the connoisseur, I have prepared a list, which is

also a vade-mecum of the kinds of chocolates that most often appear in the research of chocophiles.

Chocolates come in all shapes and flavours. One of the favourites is the chocolate truffle. These luscious sweets have a rich creamy filling that can be flavoured with champagne, rum, whisky, Grand Marnier and brandy, to name but a few. They are covered in dark or white chocolate and sometimes even rolled in cocoa or powdered sugar.

Crême fondants are usually round in shape and have a creamy filling flavoured with peppermint, chocolate, fruits such as orange, raspberry or cherry, and coffee.

Caramels are square shaped and may be plain or given an extra kick with vanilla flavouring or nuts, before being covered with milk or dark chocolate.

Nut fillings are also very popular on their own, and the most common ones are hazelnuts, brazil nuts and almonds, while chocolate 'turtles' usually contain either walnuts or pecans.

Among the other popular fillings, and almost in a class of their own, are chocolate-covered cherries – a whole maraschino cherry set in a creamy white liquor that almost drips into your mouth.

Similar in concept are candied chestnuts and stem ginger covered with dark chocolate. Though the runny filling is missing in the latter, it has a nice bite to it, unlike the very sweet cherry.

Finally, we should mention marzipan fillings. Sometimes, it is simply marzipan covered with chocolate and sometimes the marzipan is encased inside another filling, like a chocolate cream, before it is covered with chocolate.

Chocolate Tasting

The first basic element in one's fascination with chocolate is visual: its smooth, bright surface varying from the velvety light tones of milk chocolate to the dark, brilliant ones of fondant. After the visual pleasure, there is the olfactory: when you sniff it, you should smell the fragrance of good fresh chocolate, which awakens the palate. Give chocolate a decisive bite, and good-quality chocolate reveals itself by breaking cleanly and sharply with

what, in both technical and onomatopoeic terms, is a 'snap'. If, when you cut it, it crumbles and becomes powdery along the cut, it is a sign that the chocolate is too old or too dry because the amount of cocoa butter used was less than prescribed. If, under optimal conditions of temperature, that is, never above 68°F/20°C, your chocolate is faithful to the saying 'I will bend but not break', it is better left because in all likelihood it is of poor quality.

It should melt uniformly without lumps or a gritty feeling in the mouth so that you can best appreciate its velvety texture. Extra-dark chocolate, drier because it contains less sugar, should melt more slowly but still uniformly.

Milk chocolate should have more resistance when chewed but there are also certain limits here; if it stretches like chewing gum, it means it contains too much milk and too little cocoa butter; and as we all know, thrift does not help quality.

Someone who loves chocolate cannot abandon themself today to the delights of a carefully stored bar from, let's say, 1971's 'excellent vintage', because of the perishable nature of the object of their desires. There will never be auctions where chocolate is sold at astronomical prices. But kept away from light, heat and humidity (this should never be above 60–70 per cent), chocolate will last for some time, with dark chocolate lasting longest, and milk chocolate next. Filled chocolates are much more perishable.

Heat and sudden changes of temperature are responsible for the appearance of unattractive elements in the dark glamour of chocolate because they cause the cocoa butter to rise to the surface and solidify. This is efflorescence, a defect that does not affect the quality of the chocolate but does present problems for sales, especially when the chocolate is sold by the piece in shops. Putting it in the refrigerator to try and correct the problem only makes it worse. The sudden change in temperature will damage the product because it changes the crystallization of the cocoa butter and the humidity it creates coats the surface with a dry white film of cocoa butter.

CHAPTER VIII

AN IRRESISTIBLE GIFT

Here's a drink from the faraway West.
I offer it to you along with my heart,
because we must still give
descendants to the world.

Martin Engelbrecht, c1750

WHEN should you give someone a gift of chocolate? And to whom should you offer it? The answer is simple: on the same occasions as you would give flowers, or almost. There is really no time when it is not an appropriate gift to give to someone you love or to whom you want to honour or show affection or sympathy or pleasure.

A box of chocolates, especially if it comes from a good confectioner's, is a sign of good taste and generosity. A small box, elegant and tasteful, can solve the problem of giving something that is not too compromising; it is an affectionate or gallant gesture that will always be received with pleasure.

As a gift, chocolate is never inopportune or mistaken except in the case of the occasional person who is ill or diabetic. Even diabetic chocolate exists and it is more highly appreciated because the gift shows that you have given some thought to the person it is destined for – you have chosen something especially for them. Unfortunately, however, such chocolate, which I can assure you is very good and can be of help to those trying to lose weight but not wanting to give up the pleasure of their favourite sweets, is not always easy to find.

The Perfect Gift

Goethe, who adored chocolate, used to give it often and sometimes he would send with it a few tender verses to someone he loved:

You seem well disposed to me,
You smiled at my little gift.

And if only I have your favour,
Now, no sweet is too small.

Arriving at the house of friends carrying a box of chocolates is a sure way to be appreciated. However, be careful when giving a huge bar that can be broken and distributed. It should only be given to people you are very familiar with. (A child though will love it.)

To give a box of chocolates to a woman as an act of courtship is a classic gesture, but be careful with the kind of chocolates that you choose since an unknown brand with a plastic insert and an ostentatious wrapper will not win you high marks as a person of taste. On the other hand, if you choose one from a respected confectioner, and have it wrapped in a discreetly designed box, you cannot go wrong.

The perfect combination continues to be flowers and chocolates. A bunch of roses and a box of chocolates: what woman can remain indifferent before such a combination, for it is designed to appeal to all her senses. If you want to be absolutely sure of winning her affections, steal from Goethe. Use his idea of accompanying your presents with a poem, such as these words that the poet addressed to Charlotte von Stein: 'To my beloved I send flowers and sweets, so she will realize how sweet and beautiful my love is for her.'

On second thoughts, anything else is superfluous.

A famous Dutch manufacturer has designed chocolates in the shape of hearts and put them in boxes of the same shape. He sells them with the slogan, 'Melt someone's heart', and also suggests occasions, with an illustrated annotation, when this gift would be appropriate: Christmas, New Year's Day, St Valentine's Day, Easter, birthdays, anniversaries, Mother's Day, Father's Day . . . and ends with a mischievous, 'And what about today?' – an invitation to give an impromptu and spontaneous gift. For one does not need a special occasion to make such a gift. In fact, the more unexpected it is, the more gratefully it is received.

Life's Most Difficult Decision
If you have been lucky enough to have been given a box

of chocolate, according to the rules of etiquette, you should open it straight away in the presence of the giver and offer it to those present. Usually we want to do just the opposite: to take the precious box away and hide it, so we can enjoy it later in private where we can open it and eat it all by ourselves. But good manners or heartfelt generosity generally win the day and thus the gift is shared to the satisfaction of everyone. When invited to take a piece, people often start by stepping back with exclamations like 'You shouldn't let me do this . . .I'm too fat already!' or 'This is a real assault on my figure, but . . .', and then happily choose among the delicious contents of the box or tray.

Watch sometimes how, when faced with a box of chocolates that has many different kinds, the hand tentatively reaches out towards the box and then there is a moment of suspense, a small but palpable hesitation, a slight holding of the breath. In an impossibly short time one must choose just the right piece, evaluate in a glance all the different kinds of chocolates and then isolate the favourite. What we would all secretly like to do is remove the top layer so that we can see all the different kinds at once, without having to pass up a single possibility, but we know it to be impossible, and even if it were not, good manners would not permit it. So one is forced to decide quickly. Everyone has their favourites but the genuine chocolate lover chooses instinctively: that granulated coronet-shaped one is probably full of hazelnuts; and the one covered with red foil, is it coffee-flavoured or pure chocolate?

People who do not like chocolates with liqueur are always afraid they will choose one by mistake instead of those lovely chocolates filled with various layers of cream that are like a symphony of flavours on the palate. It is much better for those who like chocolate-covered cherries, because at least theirs is a more recognizable shape.

Like a seer, some people wait for a sign, divine inspiration that will direct them to the one full of mint-flavoured cream that makes them faint with delight, or that sublime rarity, marzipan and kirsch. Sometimes it works, sometimes it does not. The shiny chestnut lying serious and bare next to the two pieces with mysterious

shiny coatings hides a deceptive soul that has nothing to do with the usual filling based on marron glacé – that would be too predictable. Surprises in this field as well are neverending.

Let's look now at some of the wrappings that these lovely chocolates come in.

Less Cardboard, More Chocolate

A study made of the different boxes of chocolate would be as vast as the ocean. There are just too many kinds and models, as well as formats and packaging materials. Still, industrial chocolate, moderately priced and not particularly notable for its quality is almost always distinguished by its packaging. The long low containers are annoying, tending to be recognizable by their colours and the size of their showy and rather vulgar wrappings, with very bright cellophanes, and decorative ribbons. On the lid there is usually a sentimental picture of a cat or a landscape, flowers or puppies, shamelessly staring at us. Inside, next to the thick cardboard walls, lie layers of corrugated cardboard liners, and finally, inside paper wrappers, a few deceptive-looking chocolates. And, in spite of the thickness of a box that hints at a second layer of sweets under the first, there is only an empty space filled with more paper. This is what someone buys who hopes to make a good impression but does not want to spend any money. Usually they make an impression but it is not the one hoped for.

Chocolates from the best confectioners are just the opposite, although, of course, the price is different. Here there are two different tendencies. One is the luxuriously refined box, designed by a fashionable stylist who favours rigour as well as luxury; original shapes, mixtures of beautiful colours, natural and unexpected materials like velvet, boxes that are very hard to throw away after their contents have been eaten. The other tendency is to use a simple white or cream-coloured cardboard box, forsaking opulence to concentrate all the attention on the contents without wasting an inch of space. One layer of sweets follows another, and they manage to satisfy the most demanding and fanatic expectations. A famous Turin confectioner has always used boxes of austere simplicity for his product. Proudly exhibited in the shop window are testimonials from enthusiastic admirers and handwritten letters from famous people. A typical letter points out the richness of the contents of the simple containers the chocolates are packaged in, saying, 'Finally, a confectioner who is not deceitful', and in fact the store's advertising declares, 'We sell chocolates, not paper'.

The Prize at the Summit

There are some occasions when chocolate is absolutely the perfect thing. I think especially of trips to the mountains. I think of hours spent climbing up the peaks towards the airy summits of the snow-capped mountains and their shelters.

I remember backpacks weighing heavily on our shoulders but balancing us in the climb, heavy shirts, folded anoraks, spare pairs of woollen socks, a light but substantial picnic lunch, a flask and sugar cubes. But above all, I think of the bars of chocolate which we divided among ourselves and our guide to give us energy and reward our exhaustion.

Chocolate and sports have always gone together. But then it comes as no surprise, given the restorative powers of Theobroma.

It has always been a companion on adventures and in attempts to set records. Amundsen, the first to reach the South Pole, ate chocolate during his expedition. A famous Italian cyclist, Fausto Coppi, was a great chocolate addict and during both his gruelling training sessions and his exhausting races, as he forced himself on to victory, he always found a way to satisfy his craving.

In the Second World War, military pilots had their energy boosted with chocolate and other substances (like coca-cola for instance); today, we know some athletes use other stimulants, but for the skier or climber chocolate is still the best friend.

CHAPTER IX

CHOCOLATE AND HEALTH

Cocoa . . . is a comfort to the heart and a scourge to the brain

Paolo Mantegazza

'THE fruit of the cacao,' said the German naturalist Alexander von Humboldt, 'is a phenomenon that Nature has not repeated. There has never been such small fruit with so many qualities combined.' At the end of the age of exploration, in sixteenth-century Spain, chocolate was talked of in glowing terms. Bernal Diaz of Castillo, a historian in the service of Cortes, was one of the first when he wrote in his journal, 'When one drinks this beverage, one can travel all day without getting tired or needing to eat'.

He noted especially its effect on one's health, calling it the ideal medicine for the weak and rickety. Learned papers began to appear like 'On the Nature and the Quality of Chocolate' in which Antonio Comanero discusses the illnesses that this aromatic drink can cure. In France too the first thing that was appreciated about chocolate was its curative powers. This appreciation was carried to such extremes that chocolate came to be regarded almost as a panacea. At the end of the seventeenth century, a certain Doctor Blegny declared that he possessed a prescription 'in which those who enjoy chocolate and have the misfortune to be struck by the most universal of lovers' illnesses can find consolation'.

The therapeutic properties of the Aztec drink seemed to be limitless and around 1720 another doctor, Nicolas Audry, maintained that he could cure consumption with it. Chocolate was causing a furore in England and in the rest of Europe: that faithful chronicler of his times, Samuel Pepys, in his diaries running from 1660 to 1669, wrote that upon getting up in the morning with an upset stomach and a heavy head from abundant libations the night before, he went straight to a coffee house to drink a cup of hot chocolate and he soon found himself cured and ready to start again.

The Invective No One Listened To

Italian consumers and the medical community in the middle of the seventeenth century were not much moved by Francesco Redi's invective: 'Chocolate's not good for you/neither is tea/you'll never get medicine/like that from me.' Several decades later, a Doctor Giovanni Dalla Bona in *'Dell'uso e dell'abuso del caffe con aggiunte, massime attorno alla cioccolata ed ai rosolii'* ('On the uses and abuses of coffee and with the addition of rules about chocolate and German measles'), published in Livorno in 1762, spelled out, 'Not only is chocolate a delicious beverage but it also has medicinal properties . . . If one has a mild fever, and the temperament is phlegmatic, the humour rare, and one is approaching the age of senility, drink chocolate with a bit of vanilla, but if the temperament is bilious and sanguine, drink it without vanilla. If the humour is sour and weak, make the drink with cocoa alone, with no cinnamon and only a little sugar'.

Scarcely a year later, in 1763, Giuseppe Parini, ignoring the medicinal virtues of this delicious drink and seeing it instead as a symbol of the life of leisure enjoyed by the nobility, invited the young people of the *Giorno* to 'choose brown chocolate, given to you as a tribute by the Guatamaltecan and the Caribbean, who wear barbarian feathers in their hair'.

Puritan America also added its voice to the chorus of praises, with the president himself, Thomas Jefferson, declaring chocolate healthy and nutritious. To be completely accurate however one should mention that he was preceded a century earlier by a W Hughes who wrote in the *American Physician* in 1672 '. . . it is a tranquillizer, and excellent for relieving the pain of gout . . . it marvellously refreshes tired limbs'. He also recommends that travellers and hunters prepare some cocoa paste and sugar tablets that they can dissolve in boiling water when they need them.

Praise from the Greatest Gastronomist

In the last century, chocolate's felicitous history continued. *'Qu'est-ce que c'est que la santé? C'est du chocolat,'* declared Brillat-Savarin and, not content with that, he pointed out in *The Philosophy of Taste* that 'any one who has drunk too much from the cup of pleasure, who has spent a good part of their time at the table when they should have been sleeping, who notes that their brain is temporarily not working, who finds the air too damp and the atmosphere dificult to tolerate, who is tormented by some fixed idea limiting their freedom of thought, that person should drink a good pint of ambered chocolate'. By then, the subject was not limited to learned disquisitions, but included practical applications. In 1830, the chocolate maker and pharmacist Debauve offered the public an anti-spasmodic chocolate with orange blossom, one for 'delicate constitutions' with almond milk, and another for the 'afflicted' which was a tonic with orchid bulb – goodness only knows what that tasted like!

The Chocolate Identity Card

There have been many analyses of the composition and nutritional value of cocoa and chocolate, and the results change according to the systems of analysis and measures used. So, I will not give figures, but will limit myself instead to noting that our product contains carbohydrates, fat (in the form of cocoa butter of which the body assimilates 95–8 per cent), ash, protein (not much but it can reach as high as 9 per cent in milk chocolate), water, caffeine and theobromine.

But that is not all it is made of. It is also rich in minerals: iron (3mg per 8g in milk chocolate, 5mg in plain), calcium (in milk chocolate), phosphorus (4.55g per kilo of cocoa), magnesium (2.93g per kilo of cocoa – chocolate is the dietary substance richest in this precious metal that is so indispensible for the normal development of cells), potassium (5.63g per kilo of cocoa) and copper. Present in small doses are vitamins A, B1 and B2. The restorative function of chocolate for the nervous system is also very important, making it qualitatively superior to other exotic drinks like coffee and tea. Among chocolate's components, as we have seen, is theobromine, an alkaloid (in a 1/5 ratio) that does not directly affect the nervous system but is closely related to caffeine (0.15 per cent, such a small amount that it has no stimulating effect). Even if there is a higher proportion of theobromine, it has a much milder effect than coffee: one would have to drink at least five cups of hot chocolate to get the same effect as a small cup of coffee.

Nevertheless, people often used to rely on it as a

The famous nineteenth-century engraving, 'The Pretty Chocolate Maker'

stimulant. Napoleon, to keep himself awake when he worked out his plans, drank only chocolate. We know this because he also offered it to his secretary Bourienne who recorded the information in his journals.

In Shape with Chocolate

Chocolate is one of the foods that provides the most energy in proportion to its weight. For this reason, it is included in astronauts' diets and it is also made part of children's and adolescents' diets, as well as for convalescents, sports-people and anyone who must apply themself physically and mentally and needs a quick source of energy. 'A full pot of chocolate is more effective than a fresh egg, two ounces of beef or veal or chicken since from a pound of such meat we will never get nine ounces of such an oily and nutritious substance as we can get in cocoa,' wrote a doctor of the eighteenth century.

Depending on type, its potential calorific value varies from 480 to 800 calories per 3½oz/100g of chocolate. To be exact, it starts at one end with 293 calories per 3½oz/100g for unsweetened cocoa powder and goes up to 541 for special diabetic chocolate, to 565 for milk chocolate and reaches almost 600 for dark chocolate.

A cup of hot chocolate made with milk, sweetened or unsweetened cocoa powder, and a spoonful of sugar has 370 calories. To give you an idea of what this means, the 565 calories per 100g/3½oz of milk chocolate is equivalent to 3oz/90g of spaghetti seasoned with ¾oz/25g of butter and ¼oz/10g of Parmesan cheese. Even if your goal is to look like a piece of spaghetti, you can tranquilly replace a plate of pasta with a well-deserved hot chocolate – it is not as sinful as you thought. And if anyone reading this has real trouble resisting the temptation of just a few more pieces of chocolate, loaded with calories or not, listen to what Judith Olney affirms in her book *The Joy of Chocolate* (New York 1982): chocolate eaten in the morning is less fattening than that eaten in the afternoon. She does admit however that this is just a personal opinion and that it has never been proven.

Chocolate and Prejudices

Given the nutritious potential of chocolate, you might

think it would be hard to digest. Not true. Analyses have shown that the length of time 7oz/200g of cocoa stays in the stomach is very short, from one to two hours maximum, the same length of time as beer, wine, water, tea or coffee, even though it may seem hard to believe. Another prejudice to overcome is the idea that eating a lot of sweets – and the accusing finger is always pointed at chocolate – brings on all kinds of skin problems like acne, dermatitis, spots and even that it is the underlying cause of herpes.

To give the lie to all this, here is a report from the American Medical Association that affirms, 'Many foodstuffs must be forgiven that used to be thought of as making acne worse. Research has shown that even in large doses, chocolate has very little effect on the skin'. As far as herpes go, it has been shown that chocolate is rich in two amino acids, L-lisin and arginina, both of which have been used successfully in the cure of this ailment! But going back to acne, this tends to erupt when one eats too fast and too furiously, with a sense of guilt or anxiety, or when one turns to chocolate as a relief from stress, just as some turn to the bottle. But nothing happens when it is enjoyed calmly and with satisfaction.

You skin will stay shiny and pink, at least as much as it would with any other pleasure that you enjoy.

Another debate which is still not resolved is the relationship between chocolate and holes in the teeth. Some say that the high quantity of sugar in chocolate causes holes, but studies carried out by the Massachusetts Institute of Technology and the Forsyth Dental Center in Boston, USA, have contradicted this, at least in part. It states that 'if used in cariogenic diets, cocoa can exercise an inhibiting action. In fact, there exists an agent in cocoa which works against the *Streptococcus mutans*, the real culprit responsible for cavities'.

And what about allergies, you ask? Statistically speaking, there are fewer than you might think. Only people suffering from headaches should be careful with chocolate since it contains thiamine and can produce a bad reaction in people sensitive to it.

It seems as if the benefits of this product are limitless. Is there no one who should be careful of it? Yes. Sufferers of colitis, cystitis, gastritis and liver ailments and other such aflictions would be better staying away from its delights, with the hope that – as has already happened with the other afflictions mentioned above – medicine will discover that it has no effect on these conditions after all. In some cases, there is an escape route: for diabetics, there is a chocolate in which fructose is substituted for sucrose. Finally, a sigh of relief for those with high blood pressure: theobromine has not been found to raise blood pressure.

Happiness is a Chocolate Pudding

Science has finally confirmed what we have known instinctively for centuries: chocolate and chocolate derivatives have antidepressant pharmaceutical properties.

Unstable personalities, those lacking vital energy who are as they used to say, 'spent', look for chocolate instinctively. This is not mere coincidence. Cocoa, like all spices, grows near the equator where the sun's rays are the strongest and this is reflected in its lush plant life. But often chocolate-starved people who do not know the intrinsic anti-depressant properties of chocolate, feel guilty, and these guilt feelings get worse the more they feel attracted to the very stuff that could give them relief. It is a vicious circle.

Psychologists have noticed that the human psyche is inevitably attracted to shapes that suggest refuge, a shell, protection, that hint at a secret and precious content. It is no accident that the rose, the tulip, the snail have always fascinated us, and it is not by chance that chocolates often assumes these beautiful forms and often hide a small treasure – a hazelnut, liqueur, a cherry. Their very colour, dark and brilliant, increases their charm and attraction and stimulates an irresistible impulse to bite into their warm darkness and discover their hidden treasures, after removing their shiny foil covering. Chocolates are a foodstuff rich in symbolic meaning and value, one that can play a precise and specific role during sentimental crises as well.

Basing our opinions on medical research, comforted by learned explanations from psychologists, we can now finally indulge ourselves, aware that we will not harm our teeth, our skin or our nervous systems and, by eating chocolate, we may actually help maintain our psychological balance. With great wisdom, Charlie Brown once said, 'A good way to get over a bad love affair is to eat a delicious pudding!' He did not say chocolate but it was not necessary.

CHAPTER X

CHOCOLATE LIPS

At eleven they went to the ladies' chambers where the eight young sultanas appeared completely nude, and in that state, were served hot chocolate.

Marquis de Sade (1740–1814), The 120 days of Sodom

'THE great peace of the Florentine spring was interrupted by the uproar from the doves in the nearby dovecote beating their wings . . . In front of the window, on a little rosewood table was placed a large silver tray. On the tray, a samovar, two cups, various crystal bottles containing liqueurs, and on several little silver plates lots of little bonbons of all kinds.'

The writer of this passage who, with a feminine eye captured the smallest details of the atmosphere of the Capponcina theatre, was a noblewoman who had a brief love affair with the turn-of-the-century Italian poet Gabriele D'Annunzio. It is not difficult to imagine the lady of the moment slowly removing her glove, then choosing a chocolate, unwrapping it and languidly putting it in her mouth and savouring it with dreamy eyes while he, the incomparable lover, dazzles her with a torrent of words.

It is easy to imagine the woman who devours chocolate creams in the plush atmosphere of the Turinese confectioner's as Gozzano describes her in his poem, 'Las Golosas'.

> She raised her eyes and seemed
> to absorb with great notice
> not cream or chocolate
> but the superliquid words
> of D'Annunzio.

'. . . That night I burned with passion. I saw again all your gestures, I thought again of all your caresses. Do you remember when we got up to have a cup of milk? Do you remember the chocolate that you ate all by yourself?' This was D'Annunzio – again! – writing in a short letter to one of his many mistresses.

Certainly, chocolate has long been a weapon in the art of seduction, whether for personal consumption, or used as an aphrodisiac or a tonic. It started with Montezuma himself, who at lunch and at dinner was served no less than fifty cups of foamy *xocolatl* in gold vessels. It was said to increase his sexual vigour – and perhaps to make his more or less consenting victims capitulate.

Before facing the fatigues of the bridal chamber, Madame du Barry, the famous French courtesan, would serve it to all her lovers and Casanova offered it in much the same style that a playboy today would serve caviar and champagne.

Love and Death

But like all weapons, chocolate had a double edge: sweet or troubled according to the situation, it could inflame hearts or freeze them.

A happy couple drinking chocolate, from an early
eighteenth-century engraving by Martin Engelbrecht

In this sense the story is told of an eighteenth-century gentleman who claimed to be unsurpassable in the preparation of hot chocolate. He was so shamelessly boastful about his abilities that he wounded the pride of a woman who believed that she herself held this precious talent. Deeply offended, she took her revenge by offering him a cup of poisoned chocolate, which the unfortunate man drank to the last drop. As he felt the first fatal pains, he was still able to make one last judgement: 'Your chocolate, dear lady, would have been much better had you used a bit more sugar to hide the poison. Think about this next time.'

The Divine Marquis's Chocolate

Sade was also fully aware of the connection of love and death with chocolate, even though, as was his habit, he tended to carry things to extremes: 'An invigorating yet murderous substance, in his novels, chocolate ends up as a sign of a duplicitous nutritive economy,' wrote the twentieth-century critic Roland Barthes about him.

If on the one hand there were few orgies that did not begin with a meal and finish with a cold tonic, hot chocolate with biscuits and Spanish wine to refresh the exhausted lovers, its perverse aspect was also revealed. In fact, in the novel *Juliette*, a sleeping powder is secretly put into the chocolate drink of one character, Menski, to make him sleep and poison is put in the cups of the

young Rose and Madame Brissac to get them out of the way as well.

Chocolate for the Bishop

The use of a cup of hot chocolate as an apparently innocent but actually traitorous substance was not the prerogative only of the eighteenth century, the age of licentiousness *par excellence*. In Mexico around 1630 a cathedral in Chiapas saw the constant comings and goings of young waitresses after communion who hurried to take hot chocolate to their noble lords so they could refresh themselves. The bishop, who did not approve of this breakfast in the shadow of the altar, threatened mass excommunication. But no one paid any attention because he died shortly after, due, it was rumoured, to a cup of poisoned chocolate (privately it seems that he was a real glutton). The sweet desire to annihilate oneself or *cupio dissolvi* that anyone who passionately loves chocolate will know very well, reaches its peak with poisoned chocolate.

But there are many ways of loving and chocolate can also act as an antidote to poison. This is what happens in *The Charterhouse of Parma* (1839), when Stendhal has the lovestruck Clelia help the imprisoned hero, Fabrizio del Dongo by giving him bread and chocolate: 'Poison! Do not trust water, wine, anything; live on chocolate,' is what she counsels him.

Chocolate contains all the phases of passion – feelings of unhappiness that can only be soothed with an eager selfish taste of chocolate (while watching potential rivals with suspicious eyes) and eventually satisfaction and fullness, a delicious feeling of satiety as one rediscovers peace of mind and body.

Where there is Love, there is Chocolate

Passion for the divine food is not always so all devouring and exclusive, however. Occasionally people will decide that they are willing to offer chocolate as a gift to someone else, especially to someone they are in love with. Generosity? Have no illusions. Psychologists say that to give chocolate to someone you love almost always carries with it a hidden offer of other things . . . with, of course, an explicity sexual-erotic element.

Then there is the chocolate of our dreams: smooth, dark, voluptuous. What do psychoanalysts think of that? How do they interpret dreams in which chocolate appears? They assure us that the divine food refers to a sentimental situation for the dreamer, implying *tout court* love. This is how the unconscious sees love and chocolate. But we can console ourselves. If in a dream the emotional situation is not completely happy or it is definitely compromised, it appears as a lack of chocolate or an unfair division of it on the part of rivals, a situation which, once we are awake, we can quickly resolve by running off to the nearest shop to stock up. In reality, someone who is tormented by an unhappy love affair usually behaves in a fairly predictable way, as can be seen in a study on depression carried out by two American researchers, Donald Klein of the New York State Psychiatric Institute and Michael Liebowitz of Columbia University. There is a strong tendency for those who have been abandoned by their mate or who feel very lonely to consume chocolate. A gratifying substitute for affection, you might say, but hardly unique.

If broken hearts often feel an unquenchable desire for chocolate, there is a biochemical reason for it as well. In

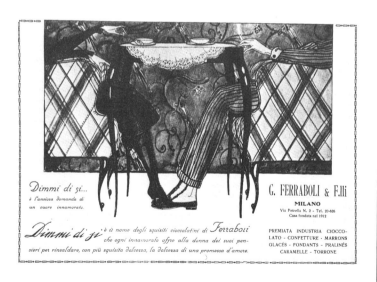

Dimmi di sì...
è l'ansiosa domanda di
un cuore innamorato.

Dimmi di sì è il nome degli squisiti cioccolatini di *Ferraboli* che ogni innamorato offre alla donna dei suoi pensieri per rinsaldare, con più squisita dolcezza, la dolcezza di una promessa d'amore.

G. FERRABOLI & F.lli
MILANO
Via Petrella N. 2 - Tel. 20-626
Casa fondata nel 1912

PREMIATA INDUSTRIA CIOCCO-LATO - CONFETTURE - MARRONS GLACÉS - FONDANTS - PRALINÉS CARAMELLE - TORRONE

states of euphoria, that is, when one is happily in love, the brain secretes in the saliva pheniletilamine, a substance similar to an amphetamine, and often referred to as an 'endogene amphetamine' because our bodies produce it directly. This substance is also present in chocolate and whoever eats it during a phase of rapid lowering of blood level (read, in cases of unhappy love) unconsciously tends to regain their equilibrium. This is what the affected Leone does in an Italian comedy *Addio, giovinezza*. As he waits for hours in the park for the young girl he is in love with, forlorn and freezing with the snow falling around him, he ends up eating the chocolates he had brought for the faithless girl. And it is a large box! 'I loved two things,' he later recalls, 'women and chocolates. Now I only love chocolate and whenever I start to fall for a woman, I go into a sweet shop and eat chocolates until I feel sick.' May he serve as an example to follow.

Wedding Chocolates

For those who are happy with their mates, what better way to celebrate it than by enjoying chocolates together?

Between 1930 and 1940 recently married Italians from Milan did not have the luxury of a full-blown honeymoon and so they had to be content with a trip to the nearby lakes. But beforehand, it was indispensible to have a cup of hot, steaming chocolate with cakes, seated in a famous old café near the cathedral. While they sipped the exquisite liquid, they would look at each other with tender eyes just like when they were courting and making so many plans for the future. A famous Milanese cook, Pina Bellina recalls, 'When I was young and newly arrived in Milan, my husband to be proposed what I though was the most romantic thing imaginable. He said "Shall we have a cup of hot chocolate together?" But it meant much more.'

CHAPTER XI
TEMPLES OF PLEASURE

To be sure of quality, you must avoid lowest
prices and patronize the best manufacturers.

Pellegrino Artusi, La scienza in cucina e l'arte di mangiar bene

WHERE are the temples to the art of chocolate
making? Where can we find famous specialities,
excellent quality, the oldest recipes and the most reliable
traditions? These are legitimate questions and every
chocolate lover has their own answers, the result of
personal preferences, their background and new
discoveries – which fortunately are still possible.

Below I offer you some of the addresses I have
accumulated over the years as I have travelled in Europe
and the United States, always on the lookout for the best
chocolate I can find.

England

Chocolate makers have traditionally prospered in
London. And, whether by chance or by intent, some of
England's best chocolate makers are clustered in Mayfair
and Piccadilly. Let's begin with a visit to Charbonnel
and Walker in the Royal Arcade at 28 Old Bond Street.
They have been selling chocolates from Old Bond Street
since 1875. One of their first important customers was
the then Prince of Wales (later Edward VII) and they
still provide chocolates for the royal family (a portrait
of the Queen can be seen inside the shop). They are
famous for their truffles as well as their rose and violet
creams. The latter have a rose-flavoured or violet-
flavoured cream filling and are covered with dark chocolate. A tiny rose or violet petal lies on top.

Prestat's is a tiny store in Piccadilly (with a branch in
Windsor) that sells excellent truffles. They also have
amusing chocolate gift items, like chocolate mice (white,
plain or milk chocolate), a big chocolate champagne
bottle with champagne truffles inside, a little tin of six
chocolate sardines and diabetic chocolate bars.

Just down the street from Prestat's is Fortnum and Mason, with a chocolate counter bound to break down all powers of resistance. Though not as old as Prestat's or Charbonnel and Walker, Fortnum's nevertheless is in the same league. The chocolate is no longer made on the premises, because they ran out of room, but one of their former chocolate makers now supplies them with all of their English chocolate and a small Belgian company also makes chocolate for them according to their recipes. They have over 150 varieties of English chocolate and over 100 varieties of Belgian. Funnily enough, it is the English who buy Belgian chocolate and foreign visitors who buy English chocolate.

A last suggestion is Bendick's in Mayfair, the place to go for bars of sport and military chocolate that delight chocolate lovers with their wonderful simplicity.

And don't despair if you are travelling abroad and you forgot to buy chocolates. Heathrow carries some of Charbonnel and Walker's chocolates for last-minute emergencies.

The United States

There is a word in the United States, 'chocoholic', which is often used as an exasperating synonym for 'connoisseur'. To say that Americans are mad about chocolate is no exaggeration. But it must also be noted that along

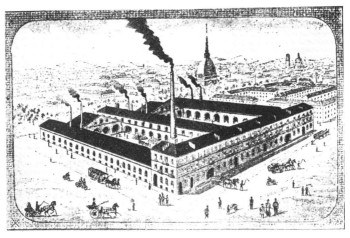

A chocolate factory at the beginning of this century

with the great mass of American consumers, all enthusiastic devourers of very sweet milk chocolate, there is a growing number with more sophisticated tastes, real connoisseurs, who in their search for the best have brought the boom in chocolate to the point of luxury. Below are some of the best New York addresses.

At Teuscher, in the Rockefeller Center, you will find the Champagne Truffle, along with eleven other kinds of truffles. Some swear these are the best truffles in town.

The famous Adrienne at Bloomingdale's offers seven equally tempting kinds of truffles. I remember especially the Jamaican with rum, the Yucatan full of the flavour of vanilla and Tia Maria, and Orangine, with a centre of orange preserve and Grand Marnier.

The Patisserie Lanciani, 275 W 4th Street, is famous for its Albino, a truffle made with white chocolate, but it also has excellent chocolates filled with coffee cream and cognac.

The lower level of Trump Tower, 751 Fifth Avenue at 56th Street, has seen several chocolate shops come and go since it opened. The latest is Swiss but they have all been good, so it is worth looking to see who is there if you visit Trump Tower.

In Le Chocolatier Manon, 872 Madison Avenue at 71st Street, you will think you have walked into a seven-

Turn-of-the-century publicity material from the Italian company, Giuseppe Majani

teenth-century lady's boudoir: there are tapestries, Venetian candelabra, a tiny desk and samples for tasting on porcelain trays. The chocolates are worthy of their setting: bunches of grapes, snails, oysters, and candied truffles and other chocolates with heavenly fillings like orange peel smothered in fresh cream, velvety marzipans and caramels that are liquid silk.

And don't overlook the chocolates sold at Saks which carries Neuhaus chocolate, or Bergdorf Goodman's tiny chocolate counter on their home-furnishings floor.

The West Coast is currently undergoing a craze for truffles too and one of the best to be found in the San Francisco area is made by Cocolat. They have seven stores now in the Bay Area, including one near Stanford University in Palo Alto. Their best-selling truffle is bittersweet, a rich, velvety chocolate made with double cream, but they have the other usual flavours like whisky and rum as well. They also sell incredibly rich chocolate desserts to take home.

In Beverly Hills, an old-fashioned chocolate shop is the Edelweiss Candy Kitchen with chocolates made by Hermann Schmid, trained in Swiss chocolate making. One of their specialities is chocolate-covered fruits, a delicious combination of tart and sweet.

If you are in Chicago, visit one of the Fannie May Candy Shops. These are not designer chocolates, but they are synonymous with chocolate to anyone who has grown up in the Midwest.

The same is true of Bailey's in Boston, though sadly there are fewer and fewer of their shops, as tastes and the cityscape change. The hot fudge sundaes are memorable, with thick, rich, chocolate fudge sauce that drips over the edge of the bowl on to the silver plate below.

And if you are ever in Hershey, Pennsylvania, you must stop and visit the Hershey Candy Company. Even as you drive into the town, the smell of chocolate hangs in the air. Imagine a town built around chocolate. Here you can visit Chocolate World which shows you how chocolate is made. There is even an amusement park with people dressed up as life-size Hershey Bars and Chocolate Kisses walking around. How can you resist a place like this?

Madness, Mania, Frenzy

Chocolate mania in America is such that – or so it seems – those not eating chocolate spend their time inventing new objects made of chocolate, perfumed with chocolate or somehow related to the world of Theobroma. In New York, for example, someone had the idea of a chocolate greeting card, the only one that will not be tossed in a corner once it has been received.

But before sending self-destructing heartbreaking messages, genuine chocolate lovers need to know everything possible about the object of their desire. And American publishers have been sensitive to their demands. They have published *Chocolate News* with paper impregnated with the scent of chocolate. It immediately begat imitations such as *Chocolatier: The Magazine for Gourmet Chocolate Lovers.*

The hunger for knowledge being insatiable, American chocolate addicts can now attend weekends for chocolate lovers organized by manufacturers and magazines. For two whole days they can abandon themselves to their passion and enjoy concoctions based on chocolate made with all kinds of different ingredients; they can listen to lectures by master chocolate makers and follow it up with a chance to express their own creativity in a cooking competition that awards the winner his weight in chocolate.

There are also chocolate sculpture competitions with hundreds of participants. In 1982 in San Francisco alone there were 9,000 'artists' signed up. But modelling objects out of chocolate is not just an American mania. In Tokyo for Valentine's Day in the big department stores they 'sculpt' a huge Venus de Milo, all in white chocolate! Of course the masterpiece does not last long; within a few hours the whole thing has been sold, in pieces.

Ah, the endless stories, where art combines with pleasure, the historical monuments, the Rolls-Royces and racing cars in all different sizes, life-size women's legs and breasts, complete sets of Monopoly and a thousand other crazy things – everything you can imagine and more. Who knows, all things considered, someday I might even find my chocolate schoolbag!

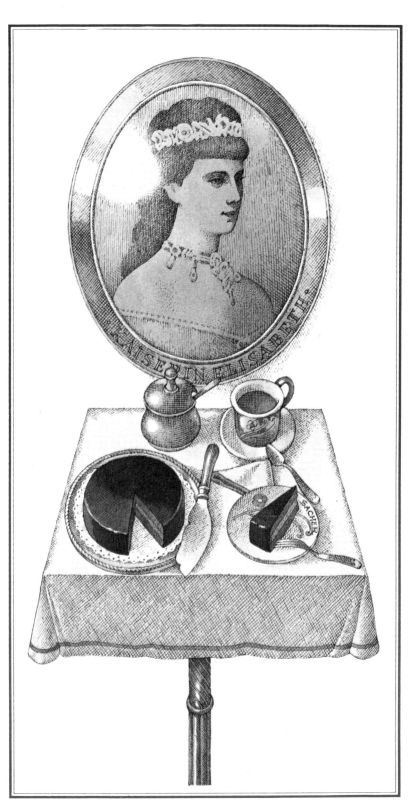

Italy

Turin is the Italian chocolate capital and so it is fitting to start there. Just passing under the arcades of the centre of town is a pleasure and it must be noted that in many of the establishments there the chocolate is excellent. A stop among the lights and mirrors of that splendid historical monument, the Baratti e Milano café on the Piazza Castello, is obligatory. Founded in 1873, it serves the best Italian chocolates, still made in the traditional way.

In Bologna, the second most important stop, one should pay a lengthy visit to the Majani establishment on the Via Carbonesi, a few steps from the Piazza Maggiore. This is the land of great traditions and here you must try the famous chocolate *scorza* (Italian for 'treebark'), with no fats and a very special consistency.

In Florence at the Rivoire on the Piazza della Signoria, the hot chocolate which used to be so famous is no longer what it once was; but as compensation, it has excellent chocolates and a delicious *gianduja* cream in a cone, which many are familiar with.

In Rome, two important addresses: the Pasticceria Svizzera-Siciliana, in the Piazza Pio XI, specializing in Sacher-type 'tortes', and the confectioner, Krechel, on the Via Frattina, frequented by dignitaries, situated as it is just behind the Palacio Montecitorio.

Switzerland

Switzerland and chocolate, two inseparable names in our geo-gastronomical world. There, every city has its confectioners and thus its chocolate, often of very high quality. In Zurich I recommend a stop at Teuscher, 9 Storchengasse; in Hefti, at the Bahnhofstrasse; in Honold in the Rennwegstrasse (excellent brandy chocolates) and finally at the Konditorei Schober, 4 Napfgasse, known for its *schokoladenlekerli* and the *pariser griottes*, or the boers.

In Berne, you must visit the Konditorei Eichenberger, 5 Bahnhofplatz, to taste the delicious square chocolates.

In Geneva, look for the exquisite kirsch-flavoured boers, and the animal-shaped specialities (the lovely cats, for example) at Rohr in either of their two establishments in the place du Molard 3 and rue du Rhone 42.

In Lugano, stop at Vannini in the Via Nassa, the street next to the lake where you may be sure that whatever you choose will be delicious.

Austria

The Austrians have a sweet tooth and they are passionate lovers of chocolate in all its forms, whether it comes in local versions (Hofbauer, Kufferle, Heller, Mirabell) or foreign. The best places in which to abandon yourself to this sweet vice are naturally the *konditoreien*, the pastry shops where tempting odours linger among gilded mirrors and plush. The selection is enormous. In Salzburg, a city famous for its *Mozart kugeln* (centre of marzipan with pistachio and nougat covered with a layer of thick chocolate), I recommend J Holzmayr in Alter Markt 7, and in Innsbruck, Murauer Gebruder, Mariatheresienstrasse 49, next to the Ritzer Konditorei and Café, at Claudiaplatz I.

In Vienna there are 450 *konditoreien*. The best is Demel, Kohlmarkt 14, the only confectioner's that makes chocolates acording to recipes dating back to 1776, the year the establishment was founded. The chocolates are kept in boxes that are in themselves works of art, but if your mind wanders amidst such a selection, you can always choose an excellent bar wrapped in sober brown paper with the two-headed eagle, symbol of the Austrian Empire. In the café of the Hotel Sacher, Philharmonikerstrasse 4, with its discreetly elegant atmosphere, they make the sachertorte according to the original recipe. Finally, a very pleasant stop is the Café-konditorei W J Sluka, Rathausplatz 8, in the centre of the Ring area, that has an incredible selection of Viennese pastries.

Germany and Holland

Lucky countries! Everywhere you go the chocolate is excellent and you can find it in all the stores and super-markets.

In Berlin, I recommend the sumptuous selections in the pastry shops of the Kadewe and Wertheim department stores. In Dusseldorf, those of the Carsch-house and Karstadt. In Munich, an obligatory stop is at the Kaffee Luitpold, in the Confiserie Rottenhoefer and at Koeppl in Rindermarkt.

In Holland, land of the exquisite Droste chocolate, I can guarantee the following addresses in Amsterdam where the selection is gratifying: Stamm, Binnemhof 29, Amstelveem; G Kremer, Damrak 65; and J Leusden, Kalverstraat.

France

The chocolate from this country is very substantial and the French have always been highly appreciative of chocolate. In fact they are proud of the fact that they have a very exclusive circle of admirers of this semi-liquid jewel, the 'Club des Croqueurs de Chocolat'.

In Paris, I can assure you of the following addresses: 44 rue d'Auteuil is only one, the most dazzling, of the six branches of Gaston Lenôtre, the very celebrated *maître–pâtissier-chocolatier*. The company makes 1,800cwt/50kg of chocolates alone, which are generally exported. The majority of the chocolates are of dark chocolate filled with hazelnuts, nougat, marzipan and orange peel.

Dalloyau at 101 Faubourg St Honoré, is an establishment that has been in business since 1802 and has kept a certain delightful *ancien régime* atmosphere. Fouquet, 22 rue François I, started up in 1842 selling marmalades and today offers thirty-two kinds of pralines, all certain to make the heart beat faster, with a clear preference for dark chocolate. La Maison du Chocolat whose head, Monsieur Linx, is a Swiss disciple of Lenôtre, is at 25 Faubourg St Honoré.

In Lyons there is another one of the temples to chocolate: the famous establishment of Maurice Bernacho at the Cours Roosevelt where the variety is incredible, but you still must try the 'palet d'or', golden tiles of dark chocolate in which are incrusted real gold *paillettes*.

Belgium

While the Swiss enjoy almost 22lb/10kg of bars of chocolate a year per person, assuring themselves of the world record, the Belgians are the biggest consumers of chocolates and pralines.

In Brussels, try Mary at 180 Rue Royal which carries the title of official chocolate maker to the Royal House and displays on gold-plated trays its exquisite sweets with their very thin coatings so one can enjoy the fillings to the maximum. Some to try are the Normandy with an unexpected vanilla- and raspberry-cream filling, the Astrid with milk and the Réjanne *amer*, dark chocolate.

The oldest chocolate confectioner's in Brussels is Neuhaus at Galerie de la Reine 25/27. The first Belgian chocolates came from its laboratories in 1857 and since then its fame has been growing. As testimony to this, there are another twenty-five Neuhaus establishments scattered around Brussels (another very good one is at Avenue de la Toison d'Or 27), not to mention the airmail shipments sent to fine shops all over the world.

At Place du Grand Sablon 12/13 is Wittamer which sells the *bouchon* in the shape of a champagne cork full of a Grand Marnier cream filling, packed in elegant brown and white boxes. The windows of Godiva are more of a visual delight than one for the palate, either at the Grande Place 22 or Chausée de Charleroi 11, where the artistic floral arrangements highlight the delicate tones of the velvet boxes containing all kinds of treats.

A Final Note

The addresses here are only a few of the masses I could have given you for your international quest for the best chocolate. Do not forget that you can also often find excellent products from the best chocolate makers in airports – all they lack is that intoxicating atmosphere of the confectioners.

CHAPTER XII
A Reader's Guide to Chocolate

WITH your permission, let us visit the house of the perfect chocolate lover. A light cloud of cocoa seems to hover in the air and we imagine hard-working hands preparing a thick smooth cup of hot chocolate to revive guests. Waiting for us on a table in the living room is a little silver tray with unwrapped chocolates, or, if you prefer, there is a dark shiny cake on a little cart, along with bottles of different kinds of chocolate liqueurs.

Raising our eyes, we are drawn to some pictures hanging on the wall. They are reproductions of the most famous paintings inspired by this delicious drink, all done around the eighteenth century, of course. Here is 'The Pretty Chocolate Maker' with her tray, and 'The Breakfast', both signed by Jean-Etienne Liotard (Swiss, of course), both domestic and sweetly serene. And then there is the morning scene painted by Longhi who portrayed the Venetian lady still in bed surrounded by a group of family members all with chocolate pots. Next the drawings from Diderot's eighteenth-century *Encyclopédie*, that show the kitchens of the chocolate maker with his tools and his helpers, the old illustrations from the first books about chocolate, botanical drawings of the magnificent plant.

On the bookshelves, the collection of books documents the alimentary properties of chocolate in studies, research, discussions, debates and recipes from the sixteenth century until today. Some of these books are listed at the end of this small contribution to the research, but there are also others less specific although no less interesting whose pages still have the faint odour of chocolate. There are important novels: *The Charterhouse of Parma* and *Buddenbrooks* (1901), as well as the lively eighteenth-century Goldoni comedies, and the Da Ponte librettos set to music by Mozart.

Among these illustrious names there also figure two more modest ones, those of the French writers Anne and

Serge Golon who invented one of the most fascinating heroines of the historical novel, Angelica, the Marquise of los Angeles, by whom even Louis XIV is captivated. In one of the long books in which she appears, she falls into disgrace at court and, looking for a new life, she becomes an entrepreneur and the first person to obtain a licence to make and sell chocolate in Paris. Given the scrupulous and passionate care that the Golons give to their research, all the passages in which Angelica and chocolate appear are very illustrative and informative. Below is an excerpt from one of them followed by a short literary anthology on chocolate. The best way to read these is to make yourself comfortable and unwrap the foil around a bar of chocolate.

The Chocolate-making Marquise

Angelica listened to the uproar that reached her from the other room, full of people. The sweet smell of chocolate mixed with that of toasted almonds penetrated the tiny office where, for two years, Angelica . . . had slaved over endless bills.

With a habitual gesture, she turned rapidly to the threshold of the room and observed 'her' customers through a discreet opening in the curtains. The day that she would become the Marquise of Plessis-Bellière she would no longer need to go into that room except when she felt like it, and then it would be accompanied by a group of young gentlemen, to savour the 'divine' chocolate. It would be quite amusing, a rather piquant revenge.

The huge mirrors with gilded frames reflected the elegantly animated atmosphere that she was able to maintain in 'The Spanish Dwarf' without great difficulty because the chocolate she served was a drink that encouraged sweet words rather than dry disputes. Very near the curtain behind which she stood hidden, she noted a man sitting alone in front of a steaming cup, melancholically opening pistachios. After looking at him again, Angelica realized she knew him and the third time she looked she began to suspect that this rather expensively dressed personage could be no one else but the policeman Desgrez, in disguise . . .

She came out of her hiding place and approached him.

'May I try to take the place – with all modesty! – of the cruel person who is keeping you waiting?'

He raised his eyes and recognized her.

'Nothing would give more pleasure than to have the owner of this fascinating place sitting with me.'

She sat down next to him, laughing, and signalled to one of her negro waiters to bring a cup and some biscuits . . .

'What do you think of this chocolate, Mr Desgrez?'

'It is truly a penance! But when you are carrying out an investigation, you know that you will be confronted with small tests of this kind. I must admit that in my work I have to go into much more sinister places than this chocolate shop.'

Anne and Serge Golon, Angelica on the Road to Versailles

Chocolate is served in the Café

EUGENIO Have you had coffee?

LISAURA No, I haven't, it is still early.

EUGENIO Do you want me to have them get you one?

LISAURA Thanks. Don't bother.

EUGENIO Bring this woman a coffee, chocolate, whatever she wants. I'll pay.

LISAURA I appreciate it, I appreciate it very much. I make coffee and chocolate at home.

EUGENIO It must be good chocolate.

LISAURA I don't mind saying, it's perfect.

EUGENIO You really know how to make it?

LISAURA My servant is a genius.

EUGENIO Would you like me to come and whip it up a bit?

LISAURA It's not worth your while.

EUGENIO I will come to drink it with you, if you
would allow me.
LISAURA It is not for you, sir.

Carlo Goldoni, The Café Shop, Act 1

Chocolate for Breakfast

Say what you will, it is pleasant to awake every morning
in a large, gaily tapestried bedchamber and, with one's
first movements, to feel the soft satin of the coverlet
under one's hand; to take early breakfast in the balcony
room, with the sweet fresh air coming up from the
garden through the open glass door; to drink, instead of
coffee a cup of chocolate handed on a tray – yes, proper
birthday chocolate, with a thick slice of fresh cupcake.
True, she had to eat her breakfast alone, except on
Sundays, for her grandparents never came down until
long after she had gone to school. When she had
munched her cake and drunk her chocolate, she would
snatch up her satchel and trip down the terrace and
through the well-kept front garden.

She was very dainty, this little Tony Buddenbrook.

Thomas Mann, Buddenbrooks

Baptism with Chocolate and Cream

A christening – a christening in Broad Street!

All, everything is there that was dreamed of by
Madame Permaneder in the days of her expectancy. In
the dining-room, the maidservant, moving noiselessly so
as not to disturb the services in the next room, is filling
the cups with steaming hot chocolate and whipped
cream. There are quantities of cups, crowded together
on the great round tray with the gilded shell-shaped
handles. And Anton the butler is cutting a towering
layer-cake into slices, and Mademoiselle Jungmann is
arranging flowers and sweets in silver dessert-dishes,
with her head on one side.

Thomas Mann, Buddenbrooks

Love and Chocolate Almonds

Perhaps even Edna did not look quite as unhappy as she

felt. It is not easy to look tragic at eighteen, when you are extremely pretty, with the cheeks and lips and shining eyes of perfect health. Above all, when you are wearing a French blue frock and your new spring hat trimmed with cornflowers . . .

An awful thing had happened. Quite suddenly, at the theatre last night, when she and Jimmy were seated side by side in the dress-circle, without a moment's warning – in fact, she had just finished a chocolate almond and passed the box to him again – she had fallen in love with an actor. But – fallen – in – love . . .

The feeling was unlike anything she had ever imagined before. It wasn't in the least pleasant. It was hardly thrilling. Unless you can call the most dreadful sensation of hopeless misery, despair, agony and wretchedness, thrilling. Combined with the certainty that if that actor met her on the pavement after, while Jimmy was fetching their cab, she would follow him to the ends of the earth, at a nod, at a sign, without giving another thought . . .

The play had begun fairly cheerfully. That was at the chocolate almond stage. Then the hero had gone blind. Terrible moment! Edna had cried so much she had to borrow Jimmy's folded, smooth-feeling handkerchief as well. Not that crying mattered. Whole rows were in tears. Even the men blew their noses with a loud trumpeting noise and tried to peer at the programme instead of looking at the stage. Jimmy, most mercifully dry-eyed – for what would she have done without his handkerchief? – squeezed her free hand, and whispered 'Cheer up, darling girl!' And it was then she had taken a last chocolate almond to please him and passed the box again. Then, there had been that ghastly scene with the hero alone on the stage in a deserted room at twilight, with a band playing outside and the sound of cheering coming from the street. He had tried – ah! how painfully, how pitifully – to grope his way to the window. He had succeeded at last. There he stood holding the curtain while one beam of light, just one beam, shone full on his raised sightless face, and the band faded away into the distance . . .

It was – really, it was absolutely – oh, the most – it was simply – in fact, from that moment Edna knew that life could never be the same. She drew her hand away

from Jimmy's, leaned back and shut the chocolate box
for ever. This at last was love!

Katherine Mansfield (1888–1923), *Taking the Veil*

Work on the Fraternidade Plantation

South of Bahia the word cacao is the only one that sounds good. The fields are beautiful when they are heavy with yellow fruit. At the beginning of each year, the *coroneis* look at the horizon and make their calculations about the weather and the crop. And then the *empreitadas* come with their workers. The *empreitada*, a kind of contract for the harvesting of a field is generally made with harvesters who have a wife and children. They agree to pick the harvest from a field and they can hire workers to help them. The workers without family do odd jobs. They work for days and do anything. With the tumblers, with the gatherers, with the receivers and on the barges. They are the majority. We earned three thousand five hundred a day but in good times it went up to five thousand reis.

A couple drink chocolate in the garden while the servant beats it; an engraving by Bonnat *c*1690

We went out in the mornings with the long poles which had small sickles on the ends of them, gleaming in the sun. And we went into the mountains for the harvest. In the field that had been Joao Evangelista's, one of the best of the plantation, a big group was working. Me, Honorio, Nilo, Valentino and some six others, were gathering. Magnolia, old Julia, Simeao, Riat, Joao Grilo and others collected and separated the pods. What remained were heaps of white pulp from which the honey trickled away. We pickers were separated from each other and could scarcely exchange a word. On the other hand, the ones who were collecting, talked and laughed. Mountains of white cacao arrived and covered everything. We put them into receptacles and left them to ferment for three days. We had to dance over the sticky pods and the sweet pulp stuck to our feet. It resisted soap and baths. Later, freed from the pulp, the cacao dried out in the sun, spread out on the barges. We danced over it there too and we sang. Our feet stayed spread out, our toes open. After eight days the cocoa hulls were dark brown and smelled of chocolate. Antonio Barriguinha took bags and bags for Pirangi, in groups of forty or fifty mules. Most of the hired workers and the *empreiteiros* only knew chocolate by that smell the cacao had . . .

Honorios, while he cut, described his ideal:

> I want a brunette,
> Who is pretty,
> Who is pretty
> with a ribbon in her hair.

The brunette never came.

Jorge Amado, *Cacao*

A SURPRISE ENDING

CHOCOLATE for all tastes and for every occasion. Chocolate moulded into bars and as a hot drink, as icecream and as a sweet, as a pudding and as a creamy spread. Something to enjoy in perfect solitude or to offer gladly to others, to munch on and to sip. But still this does not cover everything. In this triumphant parade, one auspicious object is missing – one fit for a grand finale with just the right element of surprise.

This is the chocolate egg and as for surprises, it contains several.

The first surprise is that it is rather a new tradition even though its birth date is the subject of some controversy.

A symbol of life in ancient times and later a symbol of resurrection among Christians, the egg has been a sign of spring and the reawakening of nature; for centuries it was the custom to exchange eggs as gifts during the Easter season.

At first these were hens' eggs dyed red or other colours, decorated with animal designs and inscribed with greetings and good wishes. Next in fashion came the ornamental eggs. Cast of precious metals, and embellished with enamel and gems, they were made into jewellery cases for brooches and necklaces and held the added surprise of being valuable objects in their own right. Fabergé eggs in particular were famous, products of the exquisite workmanship of jewellers to the Russian court of the Romanoffs in the last quarter of the nineteenth century, and to their descendants, right up to the eve of the Russian Revolution.

Even before that, it seems, someone at another court, that of Louis XV, had thought for the first time of covering a real egg with a layer of chocolate. No one knows why this novelty did not catch on; it was not until a century and half later that the confectionary industry took up the idea again. This time it proved a success and the chocolate egg became a classic – in fact *the* classic – symbol of Easter. Bells, doves, nests, rabbits

– the shapes of all of which are also reproduced – do not enjoy anything like the success of the egg. The egg can also be made of spun sugar or some other form of candy, but the most popular version remains the chocolate egg.

A seasonal product and a fragile one – its crafting and decoration are still done to a large extent by hand and its packaging and distribution demand special care and handling – the chocolate egg is naturally, for all these reasons, an expensive sweet. In fact, given the amount of chocolate used, it may be the most expensive of all.

Open and Ye shall Find

Those lucky enough to receive these Easter eggs are usually children, who are generally more interested in

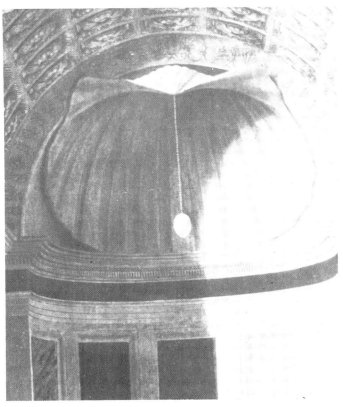

The cosmic egg, symbol of eternal regeneration, hanging in Piero della Francesca's Urbino Altar-frontal; the Pinacoteca di Brera, Milan, Italy

[109]

the surprise they contain than in the layer of surrounding chocolate. What is inside? Chocolates? Sweets? A tiny automobile or a necklace of imitation coral? A puzzle or a key chain? A tiny plush animal or a pen? Often the prize is a disappointment: the three-year-old boy who find a gadget better suited to a ten-year-old girl, who in turn finds a miniature army of plastic soldiers that she does not know what to do with. Some confectioners designate their eggs 'for boys' or 'for girls', but this does not always work either and the search goes on every year for new 'unisex' surprises.

As for the shell surrounding the egg, it is usually a very thin layer of not very high-quality chocolate, unless it was made by a reputable confectioner. But at Easter one must have the festive touch of a beautiful egg, with different colours and shiny ribbons and pretty aluminium foil. At the fateful moment when it was time to break it open in my house there was inevitably a clash of opposites. One party was patient and circumspect, building up suspense by pushing the point of the knife gently along the seam, while keeping the egg intact as long as possible in order to enjoy the gasps of surprise when it was finally opened. The other looked for the noisy theatrical gesture such as a decisive punch at the fragrant shell which had previously been stripped of its shiny covering, with the surprise teetering within the pieces of broken chocolate ready to be grabbed by greedy hands. Usually in the merry confusion that this ceremony produced, it was the second party who triumphed.

Once the eggs were broken open by their owners, there was an impatient unwrapping of the tissue paper covering the small surprises hidden within. And was this followed by cries of joy? Of delight? Not always. There was inevitably one little one, mouth full of chocolate, who would weep with disappointment.

Sometimes inside these Easter eggs people find surprises that take their breath away. They are the recipients of more personal surprises, that is, as the makers say, surprises furnished by the client. Many good confectioners will insert a special surprise inside a chocolate egg. If the recipient is a woman, when she opens the egg she will have a double surprise because she will discover that piece of jewellery glimpsed earlier through a shop window, or a ticket for the cruise she has dreamed of for years or even the ring so long awaited that says, 'Will you marry me?'

Sometimes inside these special eggs less valuable and more unexpected gifts are found, whose significance is either meant to be malicious or witty. One chocolate maker received an order for an egg to contain a beautiful orchid and it gave him a moment's pause as he considered how to enclose something living like a flower, even though it would end up encased in the most fragrant and sensual bier in the world, a superb dark chocolate egg.

The most important thing to keep in mind about these eggs *ad personam* is to send them with a tag that warns the recipient that this is an unusual egg and not – how should we phrase it – a battery egg. This is because more than once an egg, containing a surprise which had been the object of careful (and costly) search, but not properly addressed and labelled has ended up hastily recycled to a friend, a business contact or even a rival, with the resulting embarrassing consequences one can easily imagine.

The chocolate egg in any case is a fascinating present, not only for true chocoholics but also for those who like games, risk, the unknown, or a mystery. Once a year at least I want a chocolate egg. Because I love surprises.

If it is a disappointment, I eat the shell – of excellent quality of course – and that way console myself. If the surprise is a welcome one, I will enjoy my magnificent egg in celebration.

BIBLIOGRAPHY

Benzoni, Girolamo *La Historia del Mondo Nuovo*, Venice 1572

Carletti, Francesco *Ragionamenti sopra le cose da lui vedute nei suoi viaggi*, Florence 1701 (repr as *Ragionamenti del mio viaggio intorno al mondo*, Turin 1958)

Dalla Bona, Giovanni *Dell'uso e dell'abuso del caffe con aggiunte massime attorno alla cioccolata ed ai rosolii*, Livorno 1762

Fontenau, Jean-Mari *Le chocolat et sa cuisine*, Bruges 1982

Italiaander, Rolf *Xocolatl*, Düsseldorf 1980
　　Speise der Götter, Düsseldorf 1983

Jolly, Martine *Le chocolat, une passion dévorante*, Paris 1983

Olney, Judith *The Joy of Chocolate*, New York 1982

Schiedlansky, Günther *Tee, Kaffee, Schokolade*, Munich 1961

ACKNOWLEDGEMENTS

The two quotations from *Buddenbrooks* by Thomas Mann in Chapter XII are reprinted by permission of Martin Secker & Warburg Limited.